Psychology Vocabulary in Use

Anna Treger, Bronisław Treger

Psychology Vocabulary in Use

Podręcznik do nauki angielskiej terminologii psychologicznej

wydawnictwo
poltext

Recenzent
dr Agnieszka Bieńkowska

Weryfikacja językowa
Terence Clark-Ward

Redakcja
Anna Żółcińska

Projekt okładki
Marcin Górski

Adaptacja i aranżacja rysunków: Studio KARANDASZ
Ilustracje z serwisu Fotolia.com

Skład
Protext

Poltext sp. z o.o.
02-230 Warszawa, ul. Jutrzenki 118
tel.: 22 632-64-20
e-mail: wydawnictwo@poltext.pl
internet: www.poltext.pl

ISBN 978-83-7561-603-3

SPIS TREŚCI

WSTĘP

Podręcznik *Psychology Vocabulary in Use. Podręcznik do nauki angielskiej terminologii psychologicznej* został napisany z myślą o tych wszystkich, którzy powinni doskonalić swoją znajomość słownictwa, stylistyki i umiejętność wnikliwego, analitycznego czytania różnych odmian angielskiego dyskursu psychologicznego: artykułów i monografii naukowych, fachowych podręczników – ale też szkiców popularyzatorskich czy publicystycznych.

Autorzy podręcznika jako grupę docelową brali pod uwagę zwłaszcza studentów kierunków, na których psychologia jest liczącym się przedmiotem. To nie tylko – co oczywista – specjalności dedykowane tej właśnie dziedzinie, lecz także pedagogika, socjologia, filozofia i rozmaite dyscypliny medyczne. Oraz – last but not least – uwzględniali tych miłośników wiedzy psychologicznej, którzy z czystej ciekawości i pasji chcą pogłębiać swoją wiedzę, sięgając do anglojęzycznych źródeł. To również ze względu na nich podręcznik został opracowany w taki sposób, aby mógł być pożyteczną pomocą zarówno do nauki w grupie pod opieką lektora, jak i dla preferujących samokształcenie. Autodydaktom test sprawdzający, a także dokładny i szczegółowy klucz znajdujące się na końcu książki będą pozwalały na weryfikację postępów w opanowaniu materiału.

Książka zawiera trzynaście rozdziałów ogniskujących się na wybranych zasadniczych obszarach psychologii. Oprócz tekstu wprowadzającego każdy z nich mieści w sobie zestaw ćwiczeń pozwalających na opanowanie i utrwalenie kompetencji językowej w zakresie terminologii psychologicznej. Ćwiczenia są zróżnicowane. Jedne z nich sprawdzają rozumienie tekstu czytanego (pytania typu prawda/fałsz, quizy), inne to zadania wielokrotnego wyboru, uzupełnianie luk własnymi odpowiedziami, ćwiczenia ze słowotwórstwa, dopasowywanie słów do definicji/opisów i zastępowanie wyrażeń z języka potocznego terminami naukowymi. W każdym z tekstów wprowadzających i niektórych ćwiczeniach wytłuszczone zostały terminy mające kluczowe znaczenie dla danej problematyki psychologicznej.

W książce przyjęte są zasady pisowni bytyjskiej. Z podręcznika w największym stopniu skorzystają osoby, które opanowały kursy General English na poziomie średnio zaawansowanym i wyższym.

1.

THE BRAIN

Here are some brain structures in close-up.

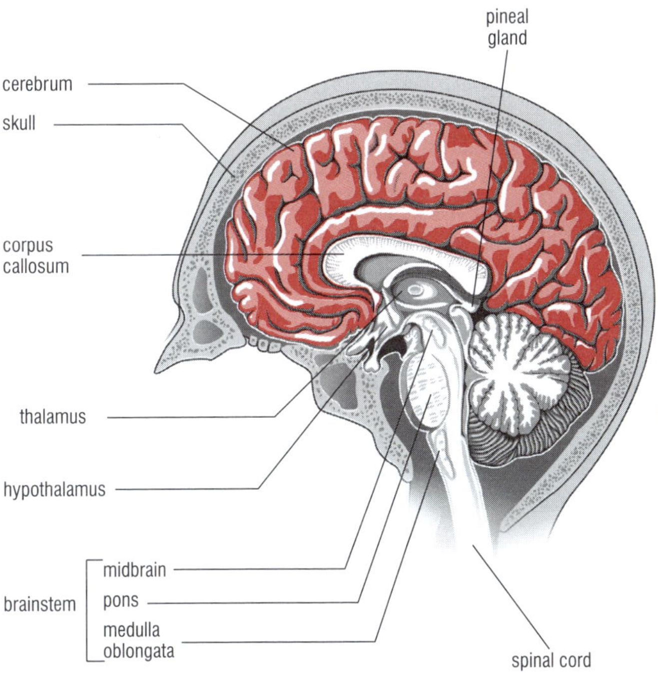

a. Parts of the brain

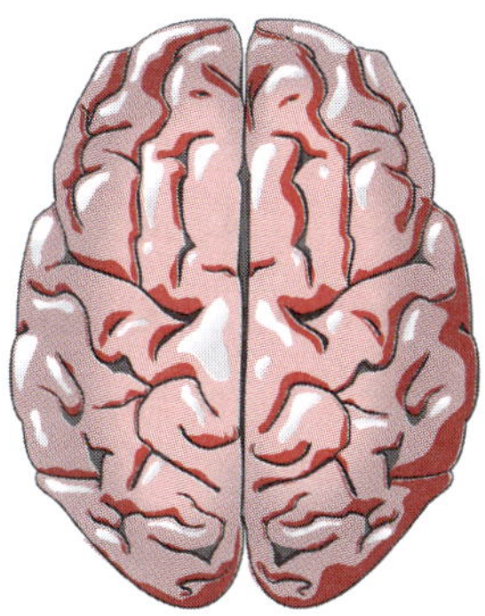

b. Cerebral hemispheres (left and right)

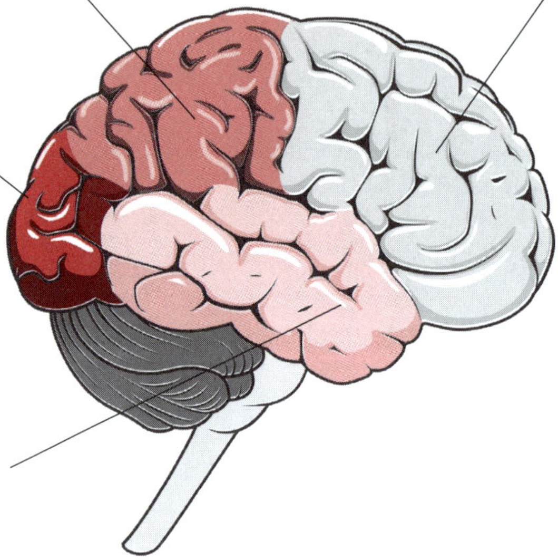

c. Lobes of the brain

Exercise 1

Read the text and do the exercise that follows.

The brain is the most complex organ in the body (in all vertebrate and most invertebrate animals), serving as a part of the **central nervous system**. The remaining part of the nervous system is **the spinal cord**. The brain is responsible for our thoughts, emotions, moods, ability to learn and remember, speech, personality, all our experiences and basic functions. Although nearly everything we do is controlled and coordinated by the brain, there are some things we don't need it to do, such as simple reflex actions.

The brain is located within the **skull** and comprises **the cerebrum**, **the cerebellum** and **the brainstem**. The brain consists of two classes of **cells**: **glial cells** and **nerve cells** also called **neurons**. Glial cells are supporting cells that provide neurons with nutrients, protection and physical support. Neurons are considered the most important cells in the brain. They are each connected by **synapses** to thousands of other neurons, forming **neural networks**. The neurons transmit information to the rest of the body through electrical and chemical signals and relate information back to specific areas of the brain, where it is processed into an appropriate response.

The cerebrum is the largest portion of the human brain. It consists of **the cerebral cortex** and several subcortical structures including **the amygdala**, **the hippocampus**, **the thalamus**, **the hypothalamus** and **olfactory bulbs**.

The cerebral cortex (also referred to as **grey matter**) is divided into left and right **hemispheres** joined together by **the corpus callosum** (a structure containing nerve fibers) and into four sections: **frontal lobe**, **parietal lobe**, **occipital lobe** and **temporal lobe**. The left hemisphere controls the right side of the body and the right hemisphere controls the left side.

The brainstem is made of **the midbrain**, **the pons** and **the medulla oblongata**.

In the course of evolution, the human brain has tripled in size and developed three distinctive layers. The brainstem and cerebellum developed first. **The limbic system** (consisting of different brain structures located on both sides of the thalamus, including the hippocampus, amygdala and hypothalamus) developed next, and the cerebral cortex developed last.

Representing only 2% of the total body weight, the adult human brain consumes about 20% of energy produced by the body.

In the past physicians and researchers had to wait until a post-mortem was performed to examine the brain. Now they can use sophisticated **brain imaging** techniques to cope with the complex anatomy of the brain without cutting it open. The most common techniques currently used include the **computed tomography scan** (**CT**), **magnetic resonance imaging** (**MRI**), **functional magnetic resonance imaging (fMRI)** and **positron emission tomography** (**PET**). When scientists want to study the structure of the brain, they use CT scanning or MRI. When they are more interested in the brain's activity, they turn to PET scanning and fMRI.

Here are the main functions of the brain structures.

The cerebrum controls higher mental functions.

The amygdala controls emotions.

The hippocampus is involved in the formation of long-term memory.

The thalamus relays sensory information.

The hypothalamus maintains the body in a balanced condition. It controls body temperature, hunger, thirst, fatigue, sleep, anger and more.

The olfactory bulbs are responsible for the sense of smell.

The cerebellum coordinates body's movement, posture and balance.

The midbrain is responsible for the regulation of vision and hearing.

The pons regulates sleep-wake cycles.

The medulla oblongata regulates basic body functions, including heart rate, blood pressure, and respiration.

Decide if the following statements are true (T) or false (F).

1. Breathing and heartbeat do not require the brain.
2. Glial cells are types of nerve cells.
3. The medulla oblongata is part of the cerebral cortex.
4. If the stroke occurs in the left side of the brain, the right side of the body is affected.
5. The human brain consumes a disproportionate amount of energy.
6. The brain and the spinal cord make up the central nervous system.
7. The cerebral cortex is the brain structure with the longest ancestry.
8. A brain autopsy remains the only way to examine the brain thoroughly.

Exercise 2

Complete the sentences using the verbs from the text in Exercise 1. Sometimes two words are possible.

1. Each part of the brain ____________ specific functions of the body that we rely on in our every-day life.

2. ____________ at the back of the brain, the occipital lobe is involved mainly in vision. Damage to the occipital lobe may result in a variety of visual problems.

3. Neural networks are ____________ from thousands of neurons connected to one another.

4. Neurons serve as the basic building blocks of the nervous system, ____________ information throughout the whole body.

5. The right side of the brain ____________ information in an emotional way, whilst the left side does it more logically and analytically.

6. Requiring a constant supply of nutrients in order to function properly, the brain ____________ much more energy than other organs.

Exercise 3

Choose the correct option.

1. A woman sustained severe brain damage in a car accident. After the accident she was no longer able to process emotional stimuli. For instance, she wouldn't be scared in a high-risk situation. Which brain structure do you think was damaged in the car accident?
   a) thalamus
   b) brainstem
   c) amygdala
   d) hypothalamus

2. Clive Wearing, an accomplished musician, has developed profound amnesia following viral encephalitis. As a result, he is not able to form new long-term memories. Which structure of the brain do you think was damaged by the virus?
   a) medulla oblongata
   b) hippocampus

c) hypothalamus

d) cerebellum

3. A man is unsteady in his movements after an injury to his brain. He is not able to walk in a straight line, and his body swaggers back and forth. Which brain structure do you think has been damaged by the injury?

   a) amygdala

   b) cerebellum

   c) thalamus

   d) corpus callosum

4. Following a head injury, a woman suffers from an impaired sense of smell. Because she has problems identifying and detecting odours, she wouldn't be alerted to foul-smelling food or to the smoke of a fire. Which brain structure do you think has been damaged?

   a) olfactory bulb

   b) amygdala

   c) pons

   d) cerebellum

5. You are out of breath after riding up a hill on a bike. Which brain structure do you think will help you regulate your heartbeat?

   a) hypothalamus

   b) thalamus

   c) medulla oblongata

   d) cerebellum

6. Andrew is often sleepy in class and doesn't comprehend much of what is being said. Which part of the brain is responsible for his sleepiness?

   a) cerebellum

   b) hypothalamus

   c) corpus callosum

   d) brainstem

7. I often wake up in the middle of the night feeling hungry. I can't fall back to sleep unless I go to the kitchen and eat until I'm full. Which brain structure makes me feel hungry?
   a) hypothalamus
   b) cerebellum
   c) corpus callosum
   d) hippocampus

Exercise 4

Choose the correct option.

From Brain Injury to Maths Genius

Back in 2002, Jason Padgett was an average Joe from the streets. He had little interest in academia and he spent every spare moment drinking in bars, hanging out at the gym or chasing girls.

Then, however, something happened that forever changed his life. On the night of September 13, 2002 Jason Padgett went out to a karaoke bar near his home and was brutally mugged. The blows he received to the *forehead/head/scalp* (1) that night left him with a *traumatic/trauma/traumatised* (2) brain injury. At hospital doctors diagnosed Padgett with severe *concussion/collision/contusion* (3), but released him the same night. Soon after the attack, Padgett discovered that he could visualise geometric shapes and physical concepts. In an interview for *Live Science* he described this experience: 'I see shapes and angles everywhere in real life.' There were downsides that came along with Padgett's new skills. Once a people person and a heavy partier, he has developed obsessive-compulsive disorder and debilitating social anxiety.

A series of brain scans that Padgett underwent revealed profound changes in the left *lobe/cortex/hemisphere* (4) of his brain and hyperactivity in the left parietal *cortex/cerebrum/cerebellum* (5) – an area that integrates information from different senses – which seems to be causing his extraordinary abilities called '*savant/prodigy/genius* (6) syndrome.'

Jason Padgett's case is an example of *neurotransmission/neurogenesis/neuroplasticity* (7), the ability of the brain to change. It shows that a brain injury can alter an individual's behaviour and personality. It also provides yet another argument in the 'mind-body' debate in favour of materialism, indicating that we are all the *work/workings/workers* (8) of our brains – all of mental life including thoughts, emotions, sensations, reasoning, and the like is the product of brain activities.

Exercise 5

Put the names of brain diseases in the correct column.

epilepsy, Alzheimer's disease, stroke, meningitis, brain aneurysm, encephalitis, Huntington's disease, brain abscess, (mild, moderate, severe) traumatic brain injury (TBI), concussion, intracerebral haemorrhage, dementia, cerebral edema, Parkinson's disease, (malignant or benign) brain tumour

BRAIN DISEASES					
Infections	Seizures	Trauma	Growth	Vascular Conditions	Neurodegenerative Conditions

Exercise 6

Complete the sentences with the names of brain diseases.

1. Her fits of ____________ occur quite infrequently, but each is scary to witness. During a seizure, she loses consciousness and has violent muscle spasms.

2. The woman's dimentia ______ first showed itself as ordinary forgetfulness. She couldn't remember simple things such as telephone numbers, but over time her condition progressively worsened until she was unable to recall her own name.

3. The patient contracted viral ____________, which damaged his brain and dramatically affected his memory. Since this point, he has been unable to recall most of his past and form new memories.

4. The boy suffered a mild ____________ after hitting his head on the ice while playing hockey. The boy was a bit dazed and confused after the incident, but he was otherwise fine. He was taken to the local hospital all the same for observation.

5. Even though brain ____________ burst relatively rarely, a rupture may cause fatal brain damage due to bleeding.

6. The man suffered a ____________ in a serious car crash that almost took his life. After brain surgery and a long therapy he was able to return to normal life, but the accident left him a changed man. Once a kind and gentle person, he became easily irritable and prone to temper outbursts at the slightest thing.

7. A 52-year-old woman was admitted to hospital with severe headaches and dizziness. An MRI scan revealed a ____________ on the right side of her brain. Luckily it was operable and the woman underwent immediate surgery to remove it.

8. Mr Baker suffered from high blood pressure, which went untreated for years mostly due to his distrust of doctors. One day he was working in the garage when he suddenly dropped to the floor. He was rushed to hospital, where his family members were informed that he had a massive ____________ .

9. Following the ____________, the man lost his speech and most of his motor skills. Given the normal pattern of recovery aided by rehabilitation therapy, he was told that he might get better in a few weeks' time.

2.

SLEEP AND DREAMS

Exercise 1

Choose the correct option.

Dreams are mental experiences, typically in the form of images and sensations that come about involuntarily in the mind during REM sleep. Dreams can be vivid, *vague/vogue* (1) or totally absurd. They can be joyful, but also very *disturbing/distorting* (2), and most people have at least one episode of waking up in the middle of the night all drenched in sweat.

While it is easy to provide a definition of a dream, why we actually dream remains one of the science's greatest unanswered questions, though it has been a topic of study dating as far back as 4000 B.C. Early civilisations saw dreams as a channel of communication with the spiritual world and in many cultures they are still believed to be mystical. To date, many theories have been offered as to what the purpose of dreaming is. According to some scientists, dreams are random and *meaningless/meaningful* (3). As psychologist Steven Pinker wrote, 'dreaming might be a kind of screen saver in which it doesn't really matter what the content is as long as certain parts of the brain are active.' However to others, dreams do make sense and serve particular functions, including memory consolidation, information processing and threat *simulation/stimulation* (4). Whatever the theory, none is yet definitive.

One of the first theorists in modern times to consider dreams was Sigmund Freud. According to him dreams were the 'royal road to the unconscious', usually relating to our *repressed/regressed* (5) emotions. He believed that addressing these emotions is a key to curing mental problems. To help people understand the meaning of their dreams, he developed the concept of manifest and latent dream content. The manifest content is the literal plot of the dream, whilst the latent content is what hides behind the plot. Although Freud's dream theories have been largely disproved, they still provoke scientists into heated debates and some people continue to believe that dreams are messages from the *unconscious/subconscious* (6) mind and look into them to gain insight into their lives.

Exercise 2

a) Match the opposites and use one of each pair to complete the sentences in b.

A	B
1. latent	a) meaningful
2. asleep	b) vivid
3. vague	c) uncommon
4. logical	d) waking
5. random	e) manifest
6. dreaming	f) repressed
7. universal	g) awake
8. conscious	h) bizarre

b) Complete the sentences.

1. My dream last night was rather ___________, but I remember particularly well a chase scene involving gun shots.
2. During REM, brain activity is similar to that of the ___________ brain.
3. Some researchers believe that dreaming is a ___________ by-product of neuronal activity during sleep.
4. Your body reacts to dreams in much the same way as if you were ___________.

5. Being chased and falling are examples of ____________ dreams that occur to most people.

6. According to Freud, ____________ content is the hidden, actual meaning of the dream.

7. Dream interpretation is a common practice in psychoanalysis used to gain insight into an individual's ____________ needs or desires.

8. As the night goes on, according to a new study, your dreams get more and more ____________ to the level of the impossible.

Exercise 3

Choose the correct option in italics in each of these sentences.

1. Scientists have shown that at various times during the night, the *sleeping/dreaming* brain is as active as when we are awake.

2. A good night's *sleep/dream* may help people find a solution even to a serious problem.

3. Adults often have *sleep/dream* imagery that relates to their waking experiences.

4. People who dream in non-REM *sleep/dream* don't usually have vivid dreams.

5. It's estimated that almost one third of the world's population suffers from *sleep/dream* disorders of various kinds.

6. Approximately, about 80% of our *sleeping/dreaming* occurs during a stage characterised by rapid eye movement.

7. One of the reasons scientists study *sleep/dreams* is to learn how people solve their problems by '*sleeping/dreaming* on it.'

8. *Sleep/Dream* paralysis is a condition in which our muscles become immobile, preventing the body from acting out our dreams.

Exercise 4

Replace the underlined words/phrases with the words from the box.

vague, recurring, repressed, random, lucid, waking

1. In Revonuso's Threat Simulation Theory, continual nightmares prepare us for bad situations in the real world.
2. Some researchers maintain that dreams are accidental projections of the brain.
3. Dreams occurring during non-REM sleep tend to be unclear and hazy.
4. During REM sleep, the brain is as active as it is during the conscious and alert state.
5. According to Freud, dreams reflect a person's hidden desires which have been pushed to the unconscious.
6. Conscious dreaming is a relatively rare phenomenon of being aware within a dream that you are dreaming.

Exercise 5

Choose the correct option(s). Sometimes more than one option is possible.

The Sleep Cycle

Sleep is a periodic state of mind characterised by reduced motor activity and suspended consciousness, in which a person in largely unresponsive to external stimuli until awaken.

When you sleep, you cycle through four stages of sleep: three stages of non-REM sleep (N1, N2 and N3) and one stage of REM sleep. Each stage of non-REM sleep can last anywhere from 5 to 15 minutes.

Sleep begins in stage 1. In this stage you sleep *mildly/lightly/gently* (1), so it's easy to wake you up. If you wake up, you may feel that you haven't been asleep at all. It is common to experience hypnic jerks, involuntary muscle *twitches/ticks/spasms* (2), during this time.

In stage 2, the body prepares for deep sleep. *Breathing/Respiration/Snoring* (3) and heart rate slow down and body temperature begins to decrease. A person in this stage needs more intense stimuli than in stage 1 to awaken.

Stage 3 (previously divided into stages 3 and 4) is where deep sleep, often referred to as slow-wave sleep, begins. The brain produces slow brain waves known as delta waves. You are less responsive to external stimuli and it is harder to *rouse/arouse/wake* (4) you during this stage of sleep. During the stages of non-REMS sleep the body repairs itself and the immune system is *strengthened/boosted/activated* (5).

Sleep does not progress to REM sleep now. After stage 3, stage 2 is repeated before *entering/approaching/reaching* (6) REM sleep. Usually, this transition is smooth, however very few children and even fewer adults experience *night terrors/sleep terrors/nightmares* (7). Technically, these are not dreams, but rather a sudden attack of fear. However frightening to witness, they aren't a reason for concern, and the next morning the child or an adult wakes up, not remembering anything of the incident. This is also the stage during which *sleepwalking/lunatics/somnambulism* (8) and bedwetting (nocturnal enuresis) may take place.

Typically, REM sleep occurs after 90 minutes of falling asleep and it accounts for about 20–25% of total sleep time. This stage gets its name from rapid movement of the eyes that accompanies it. It is also characterised by increased brain activity and heart rate. REM sleep is also referred to as paradoxical sleep because while brain activity is similar to that during *waking/walking/woken* (9) hours, the body hardly moves as most of the muscles are nearly paralysed. This is the time when most dreams occur and if you are awoken during this stage, your dreams tend to be *vivid/vague/blurry* (10). The first REM stage lasts for about 10 minutes with each recurring stage expanding.

Once REM sleep is over, the cycle begins again in stage 2. Throughout the night, it is repeated approximately 4 to 5 times until you finally wake up in the morning.

Complete the typical sleep pattern for healthy adults:

N1→ _____→_____→_____→_____→_____→_____ and so forth.

NOTE

REM is read as one word, not as a series of individual letters.

Exercise 6

Match the names of sleep disorders 1–7 with their descriptions a–g.

1. insomnia
2. apnoea
3. narcolepsy
4. restless legs syndrome (RLS)
5. sleepwalking
6. circadian rhythm sleep disorder (CRSD)
7. Kleine-Levin syndrome/'sleeping beauty' syndrome

a)
My sister suffers from this condition. She has been seen on many occasions going down the stairs in her sleep as if it were a middle of the day. Once she was found in the kitchen making herself a sandwich. Luckily, our father stays up into the early hours of the morning and steers her back to bed.

b)
Most people who have this disorder don't even know they have it, as it appears when they are asleep. They stop breathing for short periods of time during sleep due to blocked or narrowed airways. They unknowingly wake

up and fall asleep all through the night and, as a result, are somnolent during the day. My husband had gone undiagnosed for years before he finally got help. Now he sleeps with a CPAP machine, which keeps his airways open and makes him sleep better.

c)

I toss and turn in bed and can't fall asleep even if I'm very tired. And if I finally do, I frequently wake up in the middle of the night and can't get back to sleep until daybreak. So again, I toss and turn. If it weren't for the sleeping pills, I would probably never sleep through the night.

d)

This disorder is most prevalent among teenagers and young adults. Due to their nightowlish habits, they don't fall asleep until late at night and sleep in until the late morning or afternoon. When they are forced to get up early, they feel more whacked than they were before going to bed.

e)

My cousin has been diagnosed with this disorder. He has strange episodes where he becomes increasingly drowsy and sleeps long hours in the day and night. He only wakes up to eat something and use the bathroom. When encouraged to get dressed and do something, he gets aggressive and calls people nasty – something he would never do in his normal state. Each sleep episode may last days, weeks and sometimes even months. In between them, he appears completely healthy.

f)

Kate is drowsy for most of the day and has a hard time staying awake. She has periods when she suddenly falls asleep for seconds or minutes at a time regardless of where it happens without any preceding tiredness. She may doze off at work, during reading a newspaper, or even over her meals. Recently she has dropped off at the wheel, almost causing an accident. Although there are days when she manages things, her condition has seriously affected her work and home life.

g)

Viola started having these disturbing 'pins and needles' sensations about five years ago. Every night she kicks and moves her legs from side to side, unable to settle herself to sleep. She has tried everything, including prescribed sleeping pills, to ease the sensations, but nothing seems to work, except for moving her legs.

3.

SENSATION AND PERCEPTION

Exercise 1

Read the text and do the exercise that follows.

We have a multitude of **senses**. In addition to the five traditional ones, such as sight, hearing, taste, touch and smell, we have other senses, including balance, temperature, and pain, that *register* those **stimuli** that are beyond our traditional senses. The senses work together to provide different types of information about our immediate environment.

Specialised nerve endings known as **sensory receptors** located in the eyes, ears, skin and elsewhere, are *activated* by specific stimuli from the environment and from the body itself, which results in a subjective experience called **sensation**. Stimuli are *converted* or *transduced* into electrical signals by the process of **transduction** and *relayed* to the brain through nerves, where they are *interpreted* and *processed* into a cohesive and meaningful pattern, which is called **perception**.

Each sensory receptor has a particular **threshold** (or **limen**) below which it doesn't *respond* to stimuli. Therefore, to produce any sensation at all, the stimuli reaching a sensory receptor must possess a minimum intensity. Otherwise, they are too weak to be *detected*. Some of our senses, however, can respond to stimuli below the awareness threshold and interpret them outside of consciousness, a phenomenon known as **subliminal perception**. This phenomenon has become the basis for the industry selling subliminal self-help recordings that promise to help people lose weight, quit smoking, or improve their self-esteem while they sleep.

When the stimulus is barely detected, we speak of this as the **absolute threshold**. The absolute threshold is therefore a critical boundary between no response and some response. Not only does the absolute threshold vary from person to person, but also from moment to moment for the same person, depending on a number of factors, such as age, interest, fatigue, attention and expectation. In most cases, though, the absolute threshold for each of our senses is surprisingly low. For instance, under ideal conditions our vision can detect a candle flame even 50 km away and our taste allows to detect a teaspoonful of sugar dissolved in about 9 litres of water. How much larger must the amount of sugar be before you notice that the water has become sweeter? The smallest change needed for a person to tell that two things are different is called the **difference threshold** or the **just noticeable difference** (**jnd**). Our ability to detect a difference in a stimulus depends on the intensity of the initial stimulus. For example, if you hold a weight of 2 kg. and add to it another 0.2 kg., then the increase in weight is apparent. However, if you hold a weight of 5 kg., you wouldn't notice the difference if 0.2 kg. was added. It takes 0.5 kg. added to the weight of 5 kg. to make the difference noticeable. As it turns out, 'the jnd is always large when the stimulus intensity is high, and small when the stimulus intensity is low.' This concept, named after its observer, is referred to as **Weber's law**.

If you are *exposed* to a continuous stimulus for an extended period of time, **sensory adaptation** occurs, and you become less responsive to the stimulus. For example, if someone near you is wearing a perfume, the scent may smell very strong at first, but after a short time you can't notice it at all. Similarly, you feel the touch of your clothes when you first put them on, but soon you *adapt* and no longer notice them.

All senses experience sensory adaptation, perhaps with the exception of the sense of pain.

NOTE

Although both **sensory adaptation** and **habituation** refer to becoming accustomed to a repeated stimulus, they are two different phenomena. Habituation is a behavioural phenomenon, whilst sensory adaptation is a physiological phenomenon. In habituation, you can have some control over whether you notice a stimulus to which you have become habituated. Therefore, after you have become accustomed to a ticking clock, you can hear it again, if your attention is brought back to it. In sensory adaptation, you have no conscious control over a stimulus. After you have adapted to an odour, you cannot make yourself smell it again.

Decide if the following sentences are true (T) or false (F).

1. Transduction is the reception of sensory information from the environment.
2. Sensation is the process of interpreting sensory information.
3. Perception follows sensation.
4. There are no fixed thresholds.
5. We can never detect stimuli without being aware of them.
6. The absolute threshold refers to the lowest detectable level of a stimulus.
7. The difference threshold is how much something needs to change for us to notice the change.
8. The whole business has developed around the notion that subliminal messages can help people achieve their goals.
9. The ability to detect a stimulus depends not only on its intensity, but also on the state of the observer.
10. Sensory adaptation occurs when a stimulus decreases in intensity.

Exercise 2

Complete the sentences with the italicised verbs from the text in Exercise 1. Sometimes there is more than one answer.

1. By the process of transduction, environmental stimuli are ____________ into neural signals that are then ____________ to the brain for processing.
2. A stimulus must be sufficiently intense in order to be ____________.

3. Every day our senses ____________ a variety of information from inside and outside of our bodies.

4. Once the information from the senses reaches the brain, it is ____________ into what we see.

5. Sensory receptors, when ____________ by changes in the environment, send their information to the brain.

6. Under certain circumstances, we may ____________ to stimuli unconsciously.

Exercise 3

a) Match the names of the traditional senses in column A with their more formal terms in column B.

A	B
1. sense of taste	a) audition
2. sense of smell	b) vision
3. sense of hearing	c) tactition
4. sense of sight	d) gustation
5. sense of touch	e) olfaction

b) For each of the senses, write an adjectival form. In some instances, there may be more than one form. Then use them to complete the sentences below.

1. As they grow, children explore the world around them through ____________ sensations. For example, they learn about objects by putting them in their mouths.

2. If a person experiences ____________ hallucinations, his/her food may taste as if it was rotten or poisoned.

3. When an aggressive dog approaches you, your sensory receptors detect the ____________ stimuli, such as barking or growling and convey them to the brain.

4. ____________ illusions fool our brains into seeing something that's not really there, e.g. an animation instead of a still image.

5. ____________ impairment results from a range of causes, including injuries at birth, disorders (e.g. retinal degeneration), trauma, and the old age.

6. People with damaged ____________ receptors are not able to detect dangerous odours such as those from gas leaks or fires.

Exercise 4

Choose the correct option in italics in each of these sentences.

1. Individuals with *optic/optical* defects need to choose the right device for their specific needs.

2. It's not unusual for a *visually/vision* impaired person to have a few low *vision/visual* aids around the house.

3. Low *visual/vision* individuals need help other than ordinary eyeglasses or contact lenses to be able to read the fine print or to do needlework.

4. Monoculars and binoculars are *optic/optical* devices available on the market to assist short-sighted people.

5. Although at the other end of technological spectrum, aids such as audio tapes or large print reading materials can also improve *visual/vision* function.

6. Damage to the *optical/optic* nerve may lead irreversibly to total blindness.

7. *Vision/Visual* learners respond best to information they see, and not to information they hear.

NOTE

Optic and **optical** are synonyms, but they are not usually used interchangeably. **Optic** refers to anatomy (e.g. optic nerve, optic chiasm), whilst **optical** refers to sight (e.g. an optical defect) or light (e.g. optical instrument/device/aid).

Exercise 5

Complete the texts with the correct forms of the verbs in the boxes.

a) SIGHT

focus, dilate, contract, relax, constrict, project

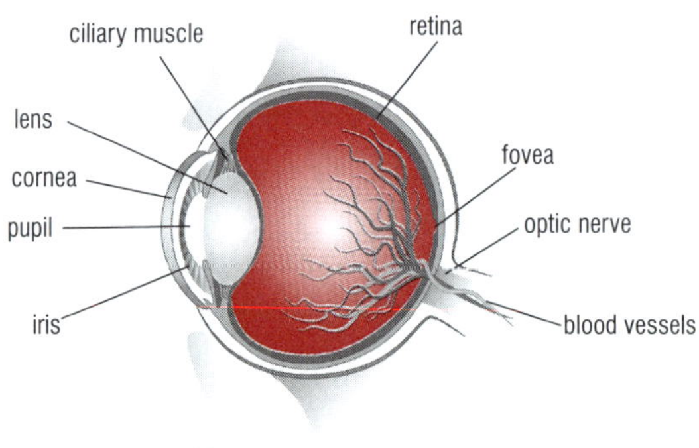

Light rays first pass through the **cornea**, the transparent, slightly bulging outer surface of the eye. From there, light enters the eye through the **pupil**. The pupil is the black opening – aperture – in the centre of the **iris** of the eye. The iris, the coloured part of the eye surrounding the pupil, consists of muscles that control the size of the pupil and thus determine the amount of light that enters the eye. In bright light, the iris ____________ (1), which decreases the size of the pupil and the amount of light entering the eye. In dim light, the iris ____________ (2) making the pupil larger to increase the amount of light. After entering through the pupil, light rays pass through the **lens**. The lens is a transparent structure near the front of the eye that ___________ (3) the light that enters the eye. The lens is attached to the eye with **ciliary muscles**, which change the shape of the lens to allow us to view an object at varying distances. When we are looking at a near object, the ciliary muscles ___________ (4) and make the lens thicker and rounded in order to focus the light rays. Conversely, the ciliary muscles ___________ (5) and flatten the lens when we are looking at a distant object.

Once they leave the lens, the light rays are ___________ (6) onto the **retina**, at the back of the eye. The retina contains different types of neuronal cells, including **cone** and **rod photoreceptors** (also known as **cones** and **rods**) and **ganglion cells**. Cones are responsible for our daytime colour vision and our ability to notice visual details. Cones are located in the central area of the retina called the **fovea**, which gives us the most detailed vision. Rods are responsible for our dim light vision and thus our ability to see in a dark place or at night. They are located outside the fovea. Cones and rods transduce light rays into electrical signals, or impulses, and transmit them to ganglion cells and ultimately through the **optic nerve** to the brain. Apart from transduction, both cones and rods are involved in dark and light adaptations, during which the retina adapts to various levels of darkness and light. You must have experienced problems with vision when entering a dark place from the bright outside (dark adaptation) or the shock to your eyes when coming out of a dark place into the bright outside (light adaptation).

Once in the brain, the electrical signals are finally processed into the visual images that you can see.

There are three basic sensations associated with vision: **hue**, **saturation** and **brightness**. Hue is the colour that we experience (e.g. red, green, or yellow). Brightness refers to the intensity of light and saturation refers to the strength or richness of the colour.

b) HEARING

strike, activate, amplify, vibrate

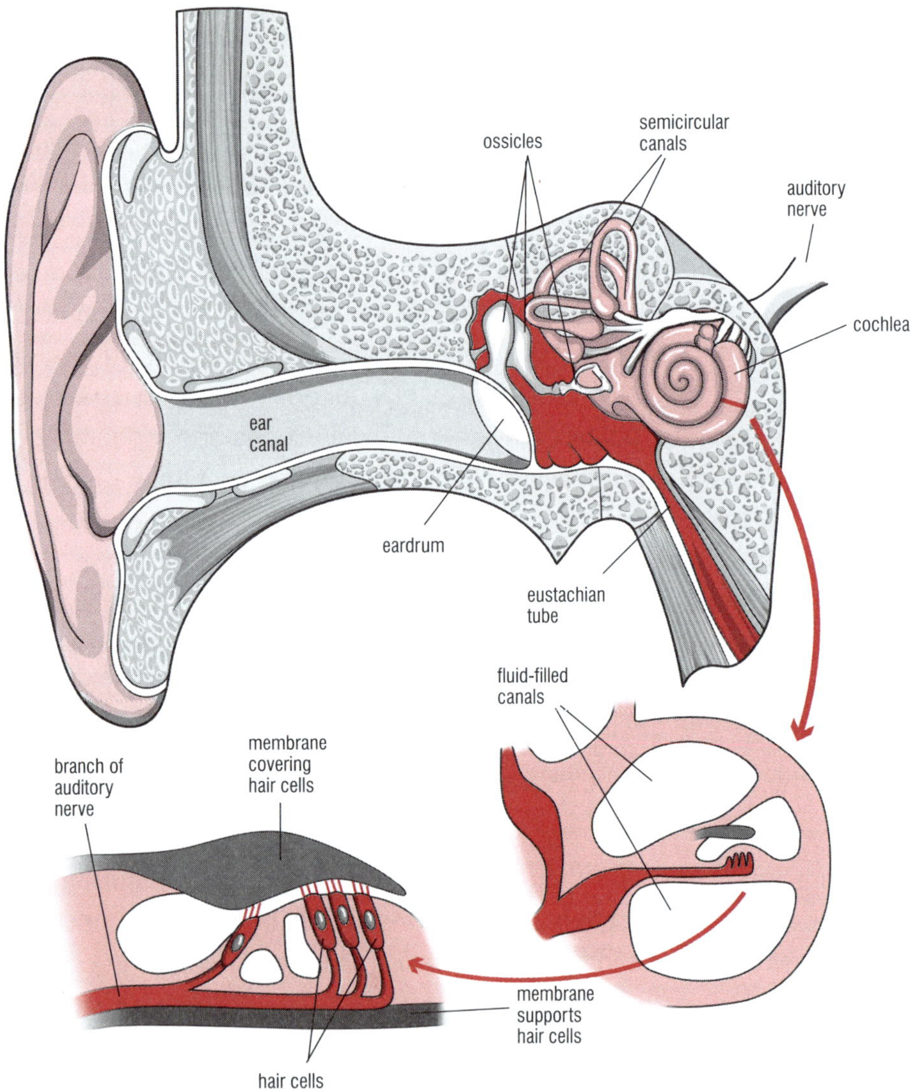

The human ear is divided into three parts: the outer ear, the middle ear and the inner ear. Sound waves enter the outer ear (called the **pinna**) and

____________ (1) the **eardrum** (or **tympatic membrane**), causing it to ____________ (2). The eardrum transmits these vibrations to three small movable bones in the middle ear (the **ossicles**): the **malleus** (hammer), the **incus** (anvil) and the **stapes** (stirrup). Each bone causes the next bone to vibrate, ____________ (3) the sound vibrations. The ossicles pass the sound through the **oval window**, a membrane to which the stapes is attached, to the **cochlea**. The cochlea is a snail-shaped structure in the inner ear filled with fluid. Vibrations of the stapes against the oval window cause the fluid to move, which in turn causes the **basilar membrane** to vibrate. The basilar membrane is a structure within the cochlea, which supports a layer of receptor cells, the hair cells. Each hair cell is topped with hairs, called **stereocilia**. The vibrations of the basilar membrane ____________ (4) these hairs and when they move, the receptor cells transduce the vibrations into electrical signals and transmit them to the brain through the **auditory nerve**. In the brain the signals are interpreted as the sounds that you hear.

Sound waves are described in terms of their physical properties: **wavelength** (**frequency**), **amplitude** (**height**) and **purity**. They produce three basic sensations: **pitch**, **loudness** and **timbre**, respectively. Pitch refers to how high or low a sound is. Higher frequency corresponds to higher pitch and lower frequency corresponds to lower pitch. Loudness refers to the intensity or magnitude of a sound, and timbre refers to the quality of a sound, other than its pitch or loudness.

c) SMELL AND TASTE

Smell and taste are anatomically different senses, yet they are so intertwined that if you lose your sense of smell, your gustatory sensations will be adversely affected. They are both **chemical senses** because they are stimulated by **chemical substances** (**odorants** for smell and **tastants** for taste). Together not only do they help in avoiding dangers (such as gas leaks or spoiled foods), but also they allow us to appreciate a wide range of **flavours** (combinations of smell and taste).

dissolve, release, produce, transport, interact

SMELL

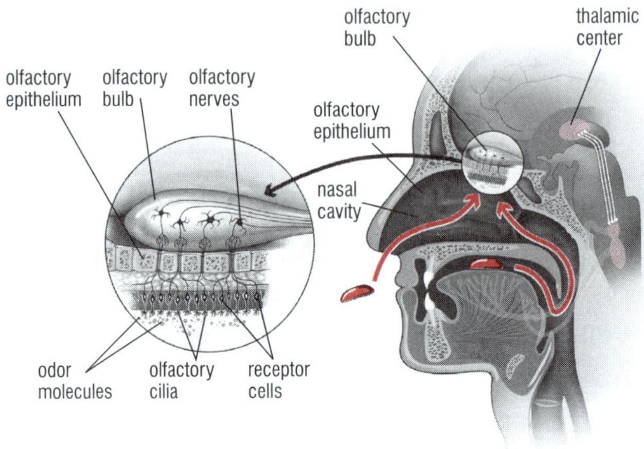

Odorants ___________ (1) odours into the air in the form of **molecules**, which enter the nose through the **nostrils**. Once inside the nostrils, the molecules travel to the **olfactory epithelium**, a small piece of skin in back of the **nasal cavity**. The olfactory epithelium contains millions of olfactory receptor cells. It is on the tiny **olfactory hairs**, also called **cilia**, at the top of each receptor cell where the molecules probably ___________ (2) with the olfactory receptor cells and, as a result, are transduced into electrical signals. These signals are transmitted through the **olfactory nerve** to the **olfactory bulb** of the brain, which then relays them to the **olfactory cortex** and from there to other brain regions. In the brain the signals are interpreted as specific smells.

TASTE

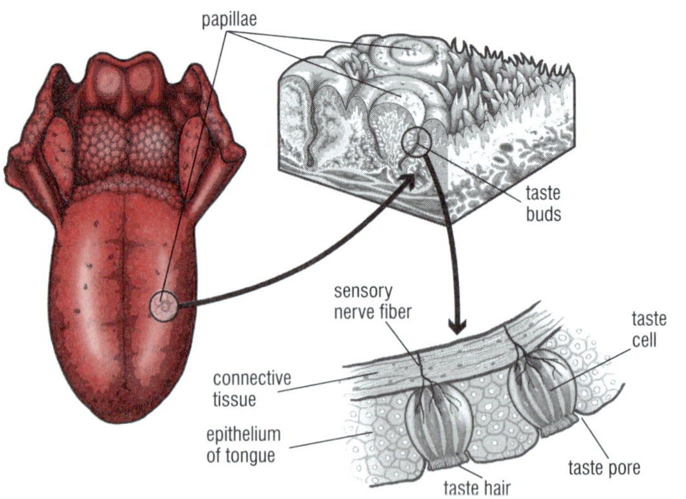

When tastants enter the mouth, their molecules ___________ (3) in saliva, a medium which ___________ (4) them to the taste receptor cells on the **taste buds**. The taste buds, in turn, are mainly located within **papillae**, the small bumpy structures on the surface of the tongue, but are also found elsewhere in the **oral cavity**, including under the tongue. The molecules interact with the taste receptor cells, which ___________ (5) four basic gustatory sensations: sweet, bitter, salty and sour. There might be a fifth sensation: **umami**, which is a Japanese word for a meaty or savoury taste. The taste receptor cells contain **gustatory hairs**, also called **microvilli**, where the actual receptors are located and where transduction takes place. Three **cranial nerves** (the facial, glossopharyngeal and vagus nerves) transmit electrical signals to the brain that interprets the flavour of what is being eaten or drunk.

d) TOUCH

regulate, regenerate, generate

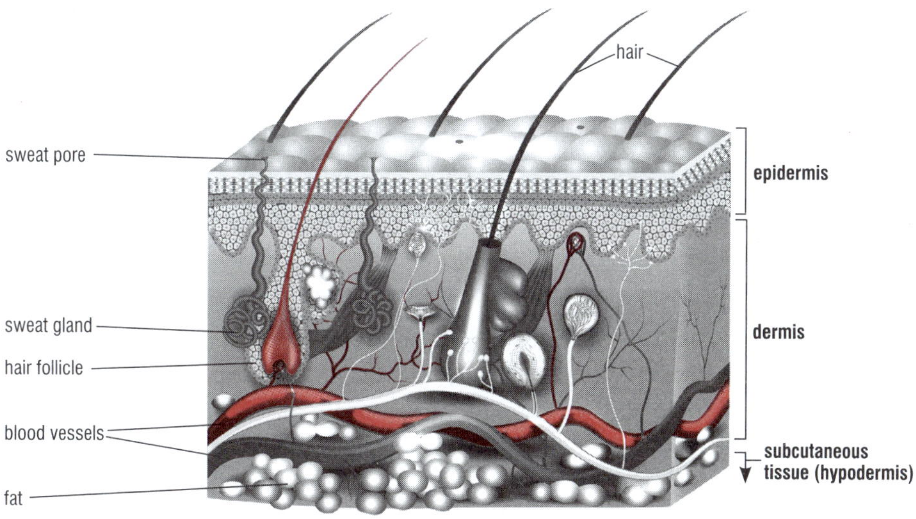

The sense of touch includes three distinct senses: pressure, pain and temperature. It originates in the skin, the body's largest organ. The skin is composed of three main layers. The very top layer, the **epidermis**, is largely composed of dead skin cells. It is constantly __________ (1) and serves as a protective barrier to harmful agents of the environment, such as UV light, abrasion or infection. The middle layer, the **dermis**, supports the epidermis and provides it with nourishment. The dermis contains numerous sensory receptors, blood vessels, sweat glands and hair follicles. The bottom layer, the **hypodermis** (also called the **subcutaneous tissue**) is primarily made of fat and connective tissue, and helps to __________ (2) body temperature. The skin contains different receptors for touch, pressure, pain and temperature, which when stimulated __________ (3) electrical signals that travel to the spinal cord and then to brain's somatosensory cortex. Because each receptor responds to different types of stimulation, different receptors are involved in stimulating the skin.

Exercise 6

Match the beginnings of the sentences with their endings, using the prepositions *through*, *into* and *to*. Use each preposition three times.

1. External stimuli enter the body	into through to	a) meaningful information.
2. Specialised cells (sensory receptors) don't respond		b) harmful environmental factors.
3. Sensory receptors transduce stimulus energy		c) sensory organs.
4. Electrical signals are transmitted to the brain		d) the air.
5. The brain interprets electrical signals		e) stimuli that are too weak to reach absolute threshold.
6. We gain knowledge of our environment		f) specialised nerves.
7. Our senses adapt		g) electrical signals.
8. Most substances release odours		h) a process known as perception.
9. The epidermis is the protective barrier		i) a stimulus that is presented continuously.

Exercise 7

Choose the correct option.

Sensing the World Through Sound

Diagnosed with retinoblastoma, a rare form of eye cancer that begins in the retina, Ben Underwood had his eyes removed at the age of three. Despite his serious ____________ (1), he never relied on any mobility ____________ (2) and yet he was able to ___________ (3) through new locations safely and lead a fairly independent life. The way he did this astonished his family, his eye doctor and everyone who ever saw him in action.

Ben Underwood was one of the handful visually ____________ (4) individuals who mastered a form of echolocation. It is the same process used in the animal kingdom, most notably by some species of bats and dolphins. Echolocating animals generate and emit sounds into their surroundings. When the sounds hit an object, they produce echoes which ____________ (5) off the object and return to their ears. Then the animals can figure out where the object is and how big it is. In the very same way, Ben was able to __________ (6) the location of objects around him and create a mental image of his surroundings. By means of echolocation, he was able to ride a bike like any ____________ (7) person, play basketball, 'hear' trees or parked cars and measure distances between them.

While many blind people listen for echoes these days, echolocation is regarded as a supplement to more conventional methods such as walking with a ____________ (8) or a guide dog. Only few individuals are skilled enough to use echolocation alone to move around.

1. a) injury	b) disorder	c) disability
2. a) aids	b) help	c) support
3. a) explore	b) navigate	c) discover
4. a) blind	b) infirm	c) impaired
5. a) return	b) send	c) bounce

6. a) discover	b) detect	c) observe
7. a) sighted	b) visual	c) seeing
8. a) white cane	b) forearm crutch	c) walking stick

Exercise 8

Read the following situations and determine which of the following terms is being referenced: *absolute threshold*, *difference threshold, subliminal perception*, or *Weber's law*.

1. You keep looking at the oncoming bus and at some point you are you able to make out what line it is.
2. In a restaurant you are served with a relatively mild dish, but still you can detect some chilli in it.
3. In the same restaurant, your partner to test your palate adds a pinch of salt to your already slightly salty soup while you are not paying attention. When you taste it, you can tell that the soup is more salty now.
4. After being on a diet for a month, your friend lost about 2 pounds. Initially, the weight loss was not enough to be noticeable, however when she lost another 10 pounds, her body started to look slimmer.
5. You want to turn the radio down. You turn the knob a little bit, but it seems just as loud as before, so you keep turning until the desired volume is reached.
6. You buy a self-help audio CD with embedded messages in the hope of losing some weight. It promises that after one month of listening you will be slimmer and fitter.
7. If the lights in your room go off, the display on your mobile phone will make the room noticeably brighter. If the lights are on, however, the display on your mobile won't really matter.

8. After the words 'cola' and 'popcorn' flashed on the screen during a commercial run before a movie, some people from the audience headed for the snack bar.

9. After a food company has changed the content of its products without informing the customers about it, you've noticed that the flavour of your favourite chocolate is somewhat bitter.

10. To check your eyes, the eye doctor shows you a row of letters through two different sets of lenses. With the second set of lenses, the letters are slightly less blurry.

11. A heavy metal group was accused of hiding a satanic message in one of their songs that could be heard when it was played backwards. Some listeners were alleged to have unconsciously perceived the evil message and acted on it.

12. If you are at a disco, you need to shout if you want to be heard. If you are in a bookstore or a doctor's waiting room, a whisper will do.

4.

MEMORY

Exercise 1

Read the text and do the exercise that follows.

In psychology, memory is a cognitive system that **encodes**, **stores** and **retrieves** information. In crude terms, encoding is breaking meaningless sensory information (e.g. sound, image, taste) into meaningful patterns that can be stored and used later. Storage refers to the retention of encoded memory over time and retrieval to recovering stored memories.

Scientists came to believe that there is no single brain structure crucial to memory. Instead, different structures are associated with memory, including the cerebral cortex, the hippocampus, amygdala, cerebellum and basal ganglia.

The **prefrontal cortex** (part of the brain's frontal lobe) is responsible for short-term memory.

The **hippocampus**, called 'the seat of memory', is considered essential for the consolidation of short-term memories into long-term ones, and for spatial memory processing. For the memory to be consolidated, it must pass through the hippocampus several times. Once it is consolidated, it is stored in the **cerebral cortex**.

The brain seems to process and store various kinds of information in different ways. For instance, declarative memory is believed to be processed in the hippocampus and the surrounding areas, whilst procedural memory in the **basal ganglia**, particularly in **striatum**, and the **cerebellum**. Declarative memory for emotional content is strongly related to the **amygdala**.

There are basically three types of memory: **sensory memory**, **short-term**

memory and **long-term memory**. Sensory memory is the shortest-term memory. It allows you to remember sensory information (e.g. visual or auditory) but only up to a few seconds. The sensory memory for visual information is called **iconic memory**, and that for auditory information is called **echoic memory**. Then there is short-term memory. Short-term memory is the storehouse of temporary information that is retained for about 30 seconds unless it's rehearsed. Its capacity is typically 7 ± 2 items. Finally, there is long-term memory, which is believed to be of indefinite capacity. It holds everything we know and remember such as skills, experiences, faces, events, songs and TV programmes. Long-term memory is divided into two subtypes: **explicit** (**declarative**) and **implicit** (**procedural**) memory. Explicit memory is the one that needs conscious and effortful recall of information. So, if you have named the capital of Slovakia or recalled the name of your high-school maths teacher, you have just made the use of your explicit memory. Implicit memory doesn't need a conscious thought though. It is the type of memory that allows you to button up your shirt or climb the stairs without thinking about it. Explicit memory can be further broken down into **episodic** and **semantic** memory. Episodic memory, as the name suggests, refers to the memory of autobiographical events such as personal experiences, emotions, places and times. In contrast, semantic memory is not related to any personal memories or experiences. It's generic memory of facts, ideas and concepts. Episodic memory which is emotionally charged is called **flashbulb memory**. This type of memory is a particularly vivid recollection of a meaningful and emotional event (such as a graduation, a wedding or a birth of a child) that will last a lifetime. Although people have great confidence in flashbulb memories, they are not always accurate in every respect. In fact, evidence suggests that flashbulb memories are no more reliable than ordinary memories.

Choose the correct answer.

1. Information fades most quickly from ____________ memory.
   a) sensory
   b) short-term
   c) long-term
   d) episodic

2. To ensure that new information is consolidated, one needs __________.
   a) retrieval
   b) storage
   c) rehearsal
   d) encoding

3. In class a teacher asks you to name the three longest rivers in the world. You answer correctly because the names of the rivers are stored in your ___________ memory.
   a) long-term
   b) explicit
   c) semantic
   d) all of the above

4. Although you are not paying close attention to what your friend is saying, you are able to recall the last few words of his utterance. It is because the brain holds the exact copy of these words in __________ memory.
   a) episodic
   b) echoic
   c) iconic
   d) semantic

5. I haven't been on a bicycle for a few years now, but after I hop back on I'm positive I'll remember how to ride. Knowing how to ride a bicycle is what's called ______________ memory.
   a) declarative
   b) semantic
   c) episodic
   d) procedural

6. At most, an average person is usually able to hold ____________ items in his/her short-term memory.
   a) 4

b) 7
c) 10
d) 15

7. Which of the following brain structures seems not to be associated with procedural memory?
   a) hippocampus
   b) basal ganglia
   c) striatum
   d) cerebellum

8. Which of the following brain structures is crucial to emotional memories?
   a) cerebral cortex
   b) cerebellum
   c) amygdala
   d) hippocampus

9. It takes you a long time to get to sleep because your mind keeps racing about the stressful events of the last few days, including a fight with your best friend. The kind of recollection that you engage in is called ________ memory.
   a) episodic
   b) flashbulb
   c) echoic
   d) iconic

10. You vividly remember where you were and what you were doing when you heard the news of the presidential plane crash in Russia in 2010. Your memory of this dramatic event is what's known as __________ memory.
    a) echoic
    b) sensory
    c) flashbulb
    d) semantic

11. You are driving along a mountainous road when a deer suddenly jumps out in front of the car and runs to the other side of the road. You see the animal for a very short time before it disappears into the thicket. The memory of the deer is briefly stored in your ___________ memory.
    a) Iconic
    b) echoic
    c) flashbulb
    d) short-time

Exercise 2

a) Complete the table with the correct forms of the missing parts of speech.

Noun	Verb
retrieval	
	retain
storage	
conversion	
	recollect
recall	
	rehearse
consolidation	
revision	
	encode

b) Complete the sentences below with the words from the table. Sometimes there is more than one answer.

1. ____________ in crude terms is a process of recovering information stored in memory.
2. It is not a secret that a good night's sleep helps us to ____________ short-term memories into long-term ones.
3. Forgetting may occur through lack of ____________ when information cannot be transferred from short-term memory into long-term memory.
4. Short-term memory has limited capacity and ____________ only seven plus or minus two elements at a time.
5. Although ____________ is a good way to strengthen memories, sometimes it's not enough to move the information into permanent memory.
6. Most events ____________ in episodic memory fade away within a relatively short time unless they are of emotional significance.
7. Sometimes information becomes ____________ into our memory without any particular effort.
8. In a history test a student uses explicit memory to ____________ the date of an important battle.

Exercise 3

Complete the following sentences with the verbs from the box in the right form.

commit, process, replay, boost, decay, discard, interfere

1. The brain ____________ the information it receives in different brain structures and in different ways.

2. It is easier for young people to ____________ things to memory than for elderly ones.

3. According to a study published in *Nature Neuroscience*, caffeine ____________ memory for information learnt the previous day.

4. The brain ____________ all the irrelevant and unwanted information to prevent information overload.

5. The sensory memory ____________ within up to a few seconds, unless it is transferred to short-term memory.

6. When new information enters memory, it may ____________ with the retention of previously learnt information.

7. The sleeping brain ____________ the experiences of the day for consolidation.

Exercise 4

For gaps 1–7 choose the answer (*a*, *b* or *c*) which you think fits best.

Supermemory

Would you like to have a perfect memory and be able to ____________ (1) reliably anything you want, anytime you want, without struggle? Think twice before you answer because while having an effortless access to memory can be blessing, it can also be truly agonising.

What is it like to have perfect recall of every single day? Nadia, a fictitious character of a House episode called *You Must Remember This*, has a super memory. She is a waitress in a busy restaurant and one day, when a woman calls for her, she is able to ____________ (2) with astonishing accuracy having served her before. She remembers everything of the encounter: how the woman looked that day, what she was wearing, what food she ordered. There are practically no gaps in her memory and it's killing her.

Nadia may be a fictitious character, but her condition is very real. People with hyperthymesia, which is the technical name for superior autobiographical memory, are able to ____________ (3) almost every day of their lives in vivid detail. Everything they see or hear is ____________ (4) in their memories forever along with bad moments. Every bad word and thought, every failure, every missed opportunity and every moment of pain goes ____________ (5). They are constantly haunted with fragments of memories. Sounds, images and scents are ____________ (6) by external stimuli, but often they return by themselves.

Some people consider hyperthymesia a gift, but not all see it that way. Sometimes ____________ (7) is a blessing.

1. a) retrieve	b) retain	c) remind
2. a) retain	b) retrieve	c) recall
3. a) remind	b) remember	c) rehearse
4. a) remembered	b) retained	c) recollected
5. a) unremembered	b) unrecalled	c) unforgotten
6. a) triggered	b) remembered	c) relieved
7. a) ignorance	b) forgetting	c) repressing

5.

MEMORY LOSS

Exercise 1

Read the text and do the exercise that follows.

We have all experienced it one time or another: a word that has escaped our memory, a misplaced key or a missed appointment. In most cases it's just an occasional **memory lapse** or **forgetfulness** that happen to people regardless of how old they are. Normal ageing may cause some forgetfulness too. It can be frustrating, but it is not a reason for concern.

A more pronounced form of memory problems is **mild cognitive impairment** (MCI), a subtle memory disorder which occurs mostly in geriatric population. MCI doesn't have to be disabling, but may be a sign of **mental decline** or the onset of **dementia**. The word 'dementia' is an umbrella term that refers to a number of **cognitive disorders**, whose major symptoms include **memory loss** or – in other words – **amnesia**. All in all, there are about 100 different types of dementia, with **Alzheimer's' disease** being the most common. Other types include **vascular dementia**, **Lewy body dementia**, **Creutzfield-Jakob disease**, and **Huntington's disease**. There are also secondary dementias that develop in later stages of other disorders such as **Parkinson's disease** or **multiple sclerosis**. Finally, there are disorders such as **Korsakoff's syndrome** that are not associated with dementia, but in which patients suffer profound amnesia.

Basically, there are two types of amnesia: **retrograde** amnesia and **anterograde** amnesia. In retrograde amnesia the brain erases memories from before the event which caused the **condition**. There are several reasons why an individual might develop retrograde amnesia. The most common is head trauma, in which there is damage to the brain regions that are engaged in memory formation such as the temporal lobe and prefrontal cortex. Other reasons include encephalitis, tumour, excessive alcohol use and stroke.

In anterograde amnesia the brain is unable to form new memories after the event. This type of amnesia usually results from damage to the hippocampus or medial temporal lobe of the brain. It may also be induced by benzodiazepine drugs, alcohol intoxication, oxygen deprivation and – less commonly – by psychological disorders.

Another type of amnesia is **childhood amnesia** (also called **infantile amnesia**). It is often thought of as normal forgetting of early childhood experiences that occurred before the age of 2–4 years. Childhood amnesia is attributable to the immaturity of neurological system, although other explanations have also been proposed.

Decide if the following sentences are true (T) or false (F).

1. In most cases, MCI interferes notably with the activities of daily life.
2. Sometimes forgetfulness may herald something serious.
3. Dementia is a specific brain disease characterised by memory impairment.
4. Both retrograde and anterograde amnesia may be caused by a blow to the head.
5. In retrograde amnesia, the individual is impaired in his/her ability to create new memories.
6. Parkinson's patients reveal cognitive difficulties from the onset of the disorder.
7. Most people lack memories of the first years of their lives.

Exercise 2

Complete the sentences with the verbs from the box in the right form.

decline, escape, erase, distort, lose, recover, form, recall, devastate, fail

1. Most people have experienced at one time or another a moment of temporary amnesia when they couldn't ____________ the right word or someone's name.
2. In anterograde amnesia, the memory of the past remains essentially unchanged, but the individual who suffers from it cannot ____________ new memories.
3. Retrograde amnesia means that the brain ____________ events from your past as a result of a head trauma or brain injury.
4. Although memory ____________ with age, it can be sharpened by employing various memory-enhancing strategies.
5. The ageing process does not necessarily ____________ memory, however it typically produces deficits in memory function.
6. ____________ your train of thought – although in all probability not a warning sign of dementia, can be very disturbing and frightening.
7. The patient ____________ most of his memories, but he still has no recollection of the car accident.
8. Over time memories become modified or ____________ because our ability to recall past events is not entirely accurate.
9. Memory ____________ us mostly because it is impermanent and requires rehearsal.
10. When a word ____________ you, don't panic. Most of the time it is mere forgetfulness, not a reason for concern.

Exercise 3

Complete the sentences with the correct terms.

1. ___________ is one of the most recognisable symptoms of dementia, alongside impairments in communication and focus.
2. ___________ such as occasionally forgetting words are no cause for concern. They are a normal part of the ageing process.
3. ___________ can happen to anyone at any age group. It can result from the most banal reasons such as sleep deprivation, stress and information overload, or more serious ones, including stroke and head trauma.
4. ___________ may be a precursor of a mind-robbing disorder such as Alzheimer's, but generally it doesn't interfere with the activities of daily life.
5. ___________ is any condition involving neurological decline and an impairment of brain functioning.

Exercise 4

Complete the sentences with the verbs from the box in the right form.

suffer, cure, progress, treat, appear, inhibit, affect, stabilise

1. Although certain medicines can ___________ patients with memory disorders, they cannot ___________ them.
2. In some people, mild cognitive impairment ___________ to Alzheimer's disease, whilst in others it remains stable.
3. Some people live to a ripe old age without ___________ from any memory-related problems.
4. Science has so far failed to effectively ___________ AD in patients with advanced symptoms.

5. For most people, the first symptoms of HD ____________ between the ages of 35 and 55 years.
6. It has been suggested that the drug could ____________ the progression of dementia.
7. Different types of dementia ____________ the brain in different ways, with the rate of progressions and symptoms varying for each patient.

Exercise 5

Read the text and choose the correct option (*a*, *b* or *c*) for each gap.

Life Without Memory

Memory is the essence of life. Without memory, we cannot have much of an understanding of our nature and the world around us. Through our experiences, it shapes our personality and makes who we are. Although it's possible to exist without memory, it's impossible to function well in society. The major breakthrough in our understanding of how memory works and where it is ____________ (1) came with Henry Molaison (best known by his initials H.M.). H.M. as a child developed, following a bike accident, a severe epilepsy. In an attempt to relieve him of epileptic seizures, a Hartford neurosurgeon conducted an experimental operation to remove a large portion of H.M's anterior temporal lobe, which included the hippocampus. The surgery was quite successful in that it reduced the patient's epileptic seizures, yet it left him with a dense memory loss. At the time H.M. was only 27 years old and his life was never again the same. His condition was diagnosed as a heavy anterograde amnesia. He was no longer able to ____________ (2) new information for more than a few minutes and he couldn't ____________ (3) explicit memories. Moreover, he suffered from a moderate retrograde amnesia and had incomplete ____________ (4) of events from the eleven-year period before the surgery.

Henry Molaison is considered the best-known and the most examined amnesia patient in the history of neuroscience, but he wasn't the only nor the most tormented by memory loss individual. There have been many others since, and Clive Wearing is one of them. Clive Wearing at the height of his career as a successful conductor and musician ___________ (5) encephalitis from herpes simplex virus which caused holes in his brain. As a result, Wearing ____________ (6) a severe case of retrograde and anterograde amnesia. His memory lasts 30 seconds at most, which means that anything that enters his mind, ____________ (7) immediately. What is more, he remembers little of the life he had prior to his amnesia.

Cases like these show us how fundamental memory is to the quality of human life. When the memory is gone, we lose our entire sense of self and, unable to move on, we are stuck in the present moment.

1. a) stored	b) retrieved	c) recalled
2. a) commit	b) retrieve	c) retain
3. a) encode	b) form	c) sort
4. a) recall	b) storage	c) conversion
5. a) sustained	b) contracted	c) underwent
6. a) developed	b) caught	c) contracted
7. a) dumps	b) erases	c) vanishes

Exercise 6

Match the types of disorders 1–5 with their descriptions a–e.

1. Creutzfield-Jakob disease
2. Parkinson's disease
3. Huntington's disease
4. Alzheimer's disease
5. Korsakoff's syndrome

a)
The patient is in her early 40s and she has been suffering from this rare genetic condition for some time now. The disorder makes her appear drunk because she staggers as she walks and makes involuntary movements. Her speech is also affected. She slurs her words and people have trouble understanding her. The disorder is taking its toll on her mind too. She is losing her ability to think and reason, and her memory is getting worse almost by the day.

b)
The sufferer who is in her late 60s has the early symptoms of this neuro-degenerative disorder. She regularly forgets the names of her children and grandchildren or where she has put her things. On many occasions she has forgotten to turn off the stove or lock the front door. She can be no longer trusted to go anywhere on her own because she may not remember how to get back home. Due to the nature of this disorder, she has trouble finding the right words or taking part in conversations.

c)
The 62-year-old patient is visibly disabled by the symptoms of this disorder. It has not yet affected his mental faculties (you may think it has because he speaks in a monotone and has no expression on his face), but his body refuses to function well. His posture has become stooped and he has a pronounced tremor in his hands, even when they are at rest. Everyday activities such as holding a teacup steady or getting out of the bed have become a challenge. He doesn't walk much now and when he does, he takes small steps and shuffles his feet.

d)
The 65-year-old woman initially showed mental symptoms such as mood swings, social withdrawal, anxiety and memory lapses, which were mistakenly diagnosed as mild depression. Later, however, they developed into physical symptoms, including jerky movements, speech impairment and seizures. As a result, her days became a series of ordeals.

This type of disorder falls under category 'sporadic', which accounts for about 85% of all cases. The remaining categories are: 'iatrogenic' (acquired through medical procedures), 'inherited' (with a family history of disease) and – the least common – 'variant' (contracted from eating beef contaminated with BSE).

e)
The patient is a 57-year-old resident of a nursing home. Due to heavy alcohol use over many years, he has lost his ability to form new memories. So, for instance, he fails to recognise a person he has met a few minutes ago or forgets why he has just entered a room. His recall of past events is also affected – it is fragmentary and discontinuous. To fill in the gaps in his memory, he makes up stories, however he believes that they are true. Aside from his memory loss, his intelligence and social skills are intact and he appears quite normal.

Exercise 7

Complete the text. The first letter of each missing word has been given.

Mrs Perry is an elderly woman who until quite recently was a fully functioning and communicative person, taking care of her adult children and grandchildren. Now, with Alzheimer's she is not the person she used to be, and never will be again.

The early symptoms of d____________ (1) began a few years ago with seemingly customary f____________ (2). She couldn't r____________ (3) important appointments, where she put her things and she had trouble finding the right word. At first her family thought nothing of it, assuming that her memory l____________ (4) were a normal part of a____________ (5). It was not until she started to feel disorientated in her own house that they realised that something more insidious was underway. Their fears were confirmed by calls from concerned family friends who also noticed that she was behaving unlike herself. Soon afterwards, a visit to a neurologist revealed a devastating diagnosis of middle-stage Alzheimer's d____________ (6). Fortunately, Mrs Perry's c____________ (7) isn't so bad that she needs round-the-clock care in a nursing home, she is being looked after in her house. There are times when she is very confused, but she can still have some good days.

6.

LEARNING

Exercise 1

Choose the correct option: *a*, *b* or *c* to complete the text.

Behaviourism is a school of thought which focuses on scientifically observable behaviours as opposed to ____________ (1) states, such as thinking and emotions. Its main influences were John B. Watson, Ivan Pavlov, Edward L. Thorndike and Burrhus E. Skinner.

The behaviourist perspective assumes that we are all born as blank slates, or tabula rasa, waiting to be written on. According to behaviourism, virtually everything a human does is regarded as behaviour and all behaviour is the result of learning through the ___________ (2) with the environment. Some forms of learning are relatively simple. For instance, with time you grow ____________ (3) to a new, loud ringtone from your mobile phone and you pay less attention to it, so you are not startled when you hear it. This type of learning is called **habituation** and it involves not reacting to stimuli that are familiar due to repeated ____________ (4). Other types of learning are more complex. One type, **classical conditioning**, involves making a ____________ (5) between two stimuli, as when you ____________ (6) some food with feeling sick and develop a strong ____________ (7) to it. The other type, **operant conditioning**, is about associating behaviour with a stimulus. It means that your behaviour is controlled and shaped through desired or undesired ____________ (8) that follow it, such as earning a reward from parents for cleaning your room or receiving a rebuke from a teacher when you are late to class.

Operant conditioning comes in four types: **positive reinforcement**, **nega-**

tive reinforcement, **positive punishment** and **negative punishment**, where 'positive' and 'negative' are not used in their basic sense. It means they have nothing to do with being 'good' or 'bad'. In the language of operant conditioning, 'positive' means that something is added, and 'negative' means that something is taken away.

1. a) internal	b) innate	c) inside
2. a) compliance	b) interaction	c) relation
3. a) accustomed	b) familiar	c) used
4. a) exhibition	b) exposure	c) encounter
5. a) comparison	b) reference	c) connection
6. a) associate	b) match	c) condition
7. a) aversion	b) allergy	c) disgust
8. a) feelings	b) causes	c) outcomes

Exercise 2

For situations 1–10, decide if the behaviour in question was acquired through habituation, classical conditioning or operant conditioning. If operant conditioning, identify which type of consequence was responsible for the behaviour (*positive reinforcement, negative reinforcement, positive punishment, negative punishment*).

1. If an inmate breaks prison rules, prison officials suspend or take away some of his privileges, such as access to the internet or an opportunity to wear his own clothes.

2. A radio is playing techno music while you study. At first, the sound distracts you and you can't concentrate. After a while, however, you adjust. The music is there, but you hardly notice it.

3. You put up an umbrella so that you don't get wet from the rain.

4. Before you start jogging, you make sure that you have properly stretched your muscles to avoid any injury.
5. A child is rewarded with a special treat each time he goes to bed without making a fuss.
6. You make a scarecrow to keep birds away from your vegetable garden. Initially the birds are scared of it, but over time, seeing that the scarecrow does no harm, they get used to it and no longer fear it.
7. I'm overwhelmed with the memories of my school trip to Italy whenever I hear the music from 'Titanic'. We often listened to it on the bus and it stirs up warm feelings for me.
8. You enter a room and feel alarmed about a loud ticking of a clock. With time, you get used to the clock so eventually you stop notice the annoying sound though it is still present.
9. A driver got flashed by a speed camera while speeding at more than 20 mph over the limit.
10. Your mother always uses the same perfume. Each time you smell the perfume, you feel safe and happy.

Exercise 3

a) Complete the table with the correct forms of the missing parts of speech.

Verb	Noun
associate	
	elicitation
reinforce	
acquire	

	exposure
	interaction
	habituation
	conditioning
punish	
	modification
reward	
	termination

b) Complete the sentences with the words from the table in the right form.

1. Peggy's two unsuccessful marriages ____________ her to avoid getting involved in a relationship again.
2. In behaviourism, learning is the ____________ of a new behaviour.
3. One of the effects of punishment is that it suppresses or ____________ an unwanted behaviour.
4. In classical conditioning, repeated pairings of stimuli ____________ a certain response.
5. Given time, we adapt or ____________ to the environment around us.
6. We use ____________, either positive or negative, in the hope of strengthening a behaviour.
7. Being ____________ to traffic noise, I've got used to it after a while and it doesn't bother me, even with the window open.
8. The woman ____________ her 5-year-old son for good behaviour by giving him a treat.

9. Pavlov's dog learnt to ____________ the ringing of a bell with arrival of food.

10. According to behaviourism, all of our behaviour is the product of learning through the ____________ with the environment.

Exercise 4

a) On the basis of the information in the figure, complete the text below.

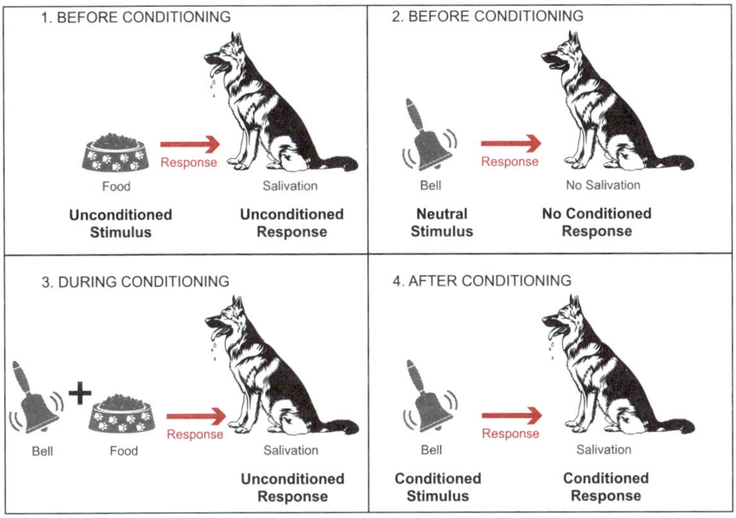

In behaviourist terms, the unconditioned stimulus elicits a natural, instinctive response. For instance, after smelling your favourite food, you may involuntarily feel hungry. In this example, the smell of food is the ____________ (1) and the feeling of hunger is the ____________ (2). The ____________ (3) is a previously ____________ (4) (the sound of a bell) that, after becoming repeatedly paired and associated with the ____________ (5) (the smell of food), alone elicits the ____________ (6) (the feeling of hunger).

b) Use the terms from part 'a' to complete the text below.

When the unconditioned stimulus is removed, the ____________ (7) decreases in strength and eventually ceases, a process known in the language of operant conditioning as 'extinction'. The conditioned response is not permanently lost, however. If the __________ (8) is again paired with the __________ (9), a __________ (10) will reappear in a weakened form. This reappearance is called 'spontaneous recovery'.

Other stimuli associated with the __________ (11) may also elicit a response in a process known as 'stimulus generalisation'. For instance, if you have been conditioned to feel hungry in response to the sound of a bell, you will also feel hungry when you hear sounds resembling a bell.

Exercise 5

a) Complete the text with the terms from the box.

fixed, variable-interval, continuous, variable, intermittent, fixed-ratio, ratio, interval, fixed-interval, variable-ratio

Schedules of Reinforcement

When reinforcement is delivered and how often it is delivered has a significant effect on our behaviour. Unfortunately, there is no single approach that can be used all the time, since what works well for one situation may not work for another. Sometimes, especially in the early stages of learning, it is best when reinforcement follows every correct response. This particular schedule is called __________ (1) **schedule of reinforcement**. It can be very effective, but it does have some drawbacks. For one thing, the response weakens or stops occurring in the absence of reinforcement. For another, the reinforcement may lose its appeal when it is used too often. In everyday life, much human behaviour is reinforced on what is called a partial or __________ (2) **schedule of reinforcement**. With this schedule, only some of the responses are rewarded.

An intermittent schedule falls into two categories. One, a(n) __________ (3) **schedule** is based on the number of correct responses. The other, a(n) __________ (4) **schedule** is based on time. Within these two types of schedules, a reward is delivered on either a regular basis, called a(n) __________ (5)

schedule or on an irregular, random basis, called a(n) __________ (6) **schedule**. Combinations of these schedules create four main types of schedules: a(n) __________ (7) **schedule,** where reinforcement is available after a specified number of responses have been made; a(n) __________ (8) **schedule,** where reinforcement is delivered after a random number of responses; a(n) __________ (9) **schedule,** where reinforcement is provided after a specified period of time has passed; and a(n) __________ (10) **schedule**, where reinforcement occurs after a random amount of time.

b) Analyse the following situations and decide what schedules of reinforcement are illustrated.

1. A teacher gives unannounced tests once in a while, therefore students must learn regularly before each class.
2. A store gives out scratchcards with every purchase that offer a free merchandise, but not every card is a winning card.
3. A coffee restaurant offers their regular customers a free drink after they have earned 20 points on their loyalty card.
4. The company rewards its salesmen with generous bonuses every month for their superior performance.

Exercise 6

Complete the sentences with the words from the box in the right form.

evoke, withhold, stimulate, increase, accustom, decrease, learn, exert, mould

1. John B. Watson claimed that he could __________ a person into anything he wanted by treating them in a certain manner.
2. In general terms, rewards __________ the likelihood of a behaviour happening again, whilst punishment __________ this likelihood.

3. Conditioned stimuli __________ strong emotions in most people, both positive and negative.

4. The behavioural perspective says that all behaviour is __________ from the environment.

5. It didn't take long for me to __________ myself to the loud chiming of the new wall clock.

6. Money, sweets and other reinforcers are all used to __________ control over our behaviour.

7. In classical conditioning, extinction occurs when the unconditioned stimulus that has been previously paired with the conditioned stimulus is __________ .

8. After repeatedly pairing the sound of a bell with the food, the sound alone __________ a dog to salivate.

Exercise 7

Match the verbs in column A to their synonyms in column B.

A	B
1. mould	a) adapt
2. reinforce	b) acquire
3. withdraw	c) evoke
4. terminate	d) strengthen
5. trigger	e) weaken
6. accustom	f) remove
7. decline	g) shape
8. learn	h) cease

Exercise 8

Complete the mini-dialogues with the correct words.

1. A: 'Can you get used to repeated loud noise?'

   B: 'Yes, but only if you are __________ to it long enough.'

2. A: 'Why did the sound of the bell __________ a salivation response in the dog?'

   B: 'Because it was paired with the food.'

3. A: 'You are making faces at the sight of milk. Do you have a(n) __________ to it?'

   B: 'I'm afraid so. Mum made me drink it once when I was sick and now I can't come near it.'

4. A: 'Is it possible to be born a criminal?'

   B: 'I don't think so. As they say, all behaviour is __________ from the environment, not inherited.'

5. A: 'Do you always reward your dog for responding to your commands?'

   B: 'Yes, that's the only way to effectively __________ his good behaviour.'

6. A: 'I've heard that Melanie is still afraid of cars. After all these years... unbelievable!'

   B: 'Yes, indeed. This single accident seems to have __________ her to fear vehicles for ever.'

7.

INTELLIGENCE

Exercise 1

Read the text and do the exercise that follows.

The nature of intelligence is one of the most complex and exciting concepts in psychology. While it has been long debated, there is little consensus among researchers on how to define it. In the popular sense, however, intelligence is the capacity to reason, have abstract thought, learn, memorise and interact with our environment. Several theories about intelligence emerged in the 20th century, the most influential including Charles Spearman's 'g' intelligence theory, Raymond Cattell's theory of crystallised and fluid intelligence, Daniel Goleman's emotional intelligence theory, Howard Gardner's multiple intelligences theory and Robert Stenberg's triarchic theory of intelligence. The theories came with questions about the nature of intelligence, whether it is **fixed** or **malleable**, whether **hereditary**, **environmental** or both. These days, there is little doubt that intelligence is both. The real debate is about how much of intelligence is hereditary and how much is environmental. Since intelligence is affected by environmental influences, it cannot be fixed. It can increase with practice and appropriate training.

Alongside the need to define intelligence came the need to **measure** it. One of the first successful intelligence tests was **developed** in 1904 by two French psychologists: Alfred Binet and Theodore Simon. Their test consisted of 30 tasks arranged in ascending order of difficulty and was meant to help teachers **identify** school children who were unable to benefit from regular classes and needed educational assistance. The score on the test (today referred to as the Binet-Simon Scale) **revealed** a child's mental age (MA). So, for instance, if a child's score was the same as the average score of children at age 6, then the tested child's mental age was said to be 6. If the child's mental age was two years ahead of his/her chronological age (CA), it meant that he/she was bright and gifted. If the mental age was two years behind the chronological age, the child was identified as needing remedial help.

After the test was developed, a psychologists at Stanford University, Lewis Terman, took it and **adapted** for use in the US schools. This new version of the test, now called the Stanford-Binet Intelligence Scale (SBIS), soon became the standard intelligence test in the USA. Unlike the Binet-Simon Scale, it **yielded** an intelligence quotient (or IQ) rather than mental age. IQ represented the ratio of a child's mental age to chronological age and multiplied by 100.

$$IQ = \frac{\textit{mental age}}{\textit{chronological age}} \times 100$$

According to this formula a child's mental age of 10 is an average score for a 10-year-old child, but it's an above-average score for an 8-year-old, and a below-average score for a 12-year-old.

The Stanford-Binet Intelligence Scale is still used today though it has been a subject of periodic revisions over the years. Currently, it is in its fifth edition.

During World War I, the military developed two additional intelligence tests known as the Army Alpha and Army Beta tests. The former was written, whilst the latter was oral in case recruits were foreign or illiterate. The tests were **administered** to assign the men to services they were considered suitable to perform. Because they proved ineffective, both the Army Alpha and Army Beta tests were discontinued soon after the war.

Further development in intelligence testing came from an American psychologist, David Wechsler. David Wechsler developed multiple intelligence tests both for children and adults: Wechsler Intelligence Scale for Children (WISC), the Wechsler Preschool and Primary Scale of Intelligence (WPPSI), and The Wechsler Adult Intelligence Scale (WAIS). His tests weren't based on IQ but on a comparison of a test taker's score to the scores of others in the same age group.

The Wechsler scales are currently the most widely-used intelligence tests. They have been **revised** approximately every ten years because of what psychologists call the Flynn effect, a theory named after John Flynn who found that IQ increases over time. As of now, there have been five editions for WISC, four for WAIS and three for WPPSI.

Choose the correct option.

1. The psychologist who proposed three types of intelligence is
   a) Charles Spearman.
   b) Howard Gardner.
   c) Robert Stenberg.

2. Among the most popular intelligence tests there are
   a) the Army Alpha and the Army Beta tests.
   b) the Stanford-Binet Intelligence Scale and the WAIS.
   c) the Binet-Simon Scale and the Stanford-Binet Intelligence Scale.

3. The Binet-Simon Scale yielded a score called the
   a) mental age.
   b) intelligence scale.
   c) IQ.

4. Binet and Simon developed a test in order to
   a) identify students who needed special help in school.
   b) identify students who were too slow to attend school.
   c) both a and b.

5. On the Binet-Simon Scale, children went through 30 items of increasing difficulty.
   a) True
   b) False
   c) It is not mentioned.

6. What is the relation between Stanford-Binet Intelligence Scale and Binet-Simon Scale?
   a) They were both co-authored by Alfred Binet.

b) The Binet-Simon Scale is a revised version of the Stanford-Binet Intelligence Scale.

c) The Stanford-Binet Intelligence Scale is a descendant of the Binet-Simon Scale.

7. According to Binet and Simon, a 10-year old child who answers correctly the questions usually answered by 10-year-olds has a mental age

a) of 10.

b) of 100.

c) below 10.

8. A boy passed more tasks on the Stanford-Binet Scale than a girl, yet his IQ score was lower. How was it possible?

a) The boy was younger than the girl.

b) The girl was younger than the boy.

c) It was not possible.

9. If the mental age is the same as the chronological age, then

a) the IQ equals 100.

b) a test taker is of average intelligence.

c) both a and b

10. IQ tests are regularly ________ to ensure that they accurately assess test takers' cognitive abilities.

a) replaced by other tests

b) updated

c) both a and b

11. During World War II, about 2 million recruits were tested with either the Army Alpha or the Army Beta.

a) True

b) False

c) It is not mentioned.

12. Scores of test takers on Wechsler's tests are
    a) derived from dividing mental age by chronological age.
    b) the ratio of mental to chronological age multiplied by 100.
    c) compared to scores of other test takers of the same age.

Exercise 2

Complete the sentences below with the verbs from the box in the right form.

measure, determine, predict, identify, focus, yield, reflect, differentiate, stream, label, neglect

1. Charles Spearman's 'g' intelligence theory asserts that intelligence is __________ on a single, main component.
2. IQ tests are meant to __________ people's intelligence and classify them according to the scores obtained.
3. Some psychologists argue that traditional IQ tests don't __________ the complete picture of a person's intelligence as they test only in certain areas.
4. IQ tests __________ people with regard to their cognitive skills.
5. Since 1960s IQ tests have been criticised as being culturally biased and __________ creative and practical abilities.
6. The positive aspect of IQ testing is that intelligence tests can __________ children with special needs. The negative aspect is that they may __________ less gifted students as slow.
7. Dividing a test taker's mental age by his/her chronological age and multiplying the score by the number 100, __________ an intelligence quotient.
8. A substantial body of research shows that both heredity and environment play a role in __________ IQ.

9. Binet-Simon Intelligence Scale helped __________ children according to their abilities and aptitudes.

10. In spite of many limitations, IQ tests can __________ children's academic performance.

Exercise 3

Complete the sentences below with the nouns from the box.

composite, hallmarks, make-up, quotient, indicator, entity, ratio, capacities

1. Through their intelligence humans possess the cognitive __________ to understand, learn, reason, memorise and solve problems.

2. According to Robert Stenberg, intelligence is not a single ability but a __________ of analytical, creative and practical intelligences.

3. Some people look at intelligence as a fixed __________ which is innate – predetermined by your genetic __________, and cannot be changed.

4. IQ is said to be a(n) __________ of an individual's intelligence, however it's not a perfect measure.

5. Ability to learn, memorise, reason, plan and solve problems are __________ of intelligence.

6. IQ is calculated as the __________ of a test taker's mental age to chronological age, multiplied by 100.

7. Intelligence __________ is a score that an individual gets on an intelligence tests.

Exercise 4

Complete the sentences with the verbs from the box in the right form.

revise, develop, adapt, discontinue, administer, misuse

1. The earliest IQ tests were __________ by Alfred Binet and Theodore Simon.
2. IQ tests can be __________ both individually and in groups.
3. Binet-Simon Scale was later __________ by Lewis Terman for use in the USA.
4. Intelligence tests are periodically __________ to keep the content appropriate and up to date.
5. IQ tests are __________ when they put culturally and racially diverse children at a disadvantage only because they haven't developed the knowledge and skills required for these tests.
6. The Alpha and Beta army tests were __________ once World War I ended.

8. PERSONALITY

Exercise 1

Read the text and do the exercise that follows.

Most people usually think of personality as a set of external appearances (actions). Even a person's body language and the tone of voice can be an indicator of personality. In philosophy, personality is the sense of the self. As a psychological concept, however, personality is seen as a combination of unique and relatively consistent emotional, cognitive and behavioural **traits** that differentiate one person from another throughout life. In short, it's the total quality of an individual's behaviour. How an individual acquires these traits is a topic of interest for many experts in the field of personality development.

Psychologists differ in their approaches to human personality. From their efforts a number of theories have emerged over the years to explain the complexity of human nature. The theories look at a person from different perspectives and as such they complement, rather than contradict, one another. Two of the most influential and interesting are Freud's **psychoanalytic theory** and Bandura's **social cognitive theory**.

According to Freud's psychoanalytic theory, personality development goes through a series of five stages, each associated with a particular **erogenous zone** of the body. At each stage, there is a crisis which must be resolved. If it is not resolved successfully, an individual becomes **fixated** at it.

The first developmental stage (0–18 months) is called the **oral stage**. During this stage the mouth is the main source of pleasure. Personality problems arise when a child is either too early or too late weaned from breastfeeding. Early weaning may create hostile and cynical adults who cope with problems in an orally aggressive manner, e.g. shouting or swearing. Delayed weaning may result in a personality that is overly dependent on others and needy. Other orally fixated activities include bad habits such as overeating, nail biting, alcohol abuse, smoking or talkativeness.

Next is the **anal stage** (18 months–3 years). In the anal stage the anus becomes the centre of pleasure. A crucial aspect of this stage is **toilet training** and problems may emerge when toilet training is not handled properly. If **fixation** occurs from too harsh or too early toilet-training, it may lead to stinginess or excessive neatness later in life. If fixation occurs from too lax or too late toilet-training, it may produce impulsive, messy or disorganised adults.

The next stage is the **phallic stage** (3–6 years). The focus of pleasure moves from the anus to the phallus. The major conflict that children experience during this stage is about their object of their sexual fantasies. The boy unconsciously falls in love with his mother, and the girl with her father. For the boy, the phenomenon is called the **Oedipus complex**, and for the girl, the **Electra complex** (Freud rejected this concept in his later writings). The boy's fear of his father makes him eventually repress his sexual desires and leads him to identify with his father. Fixation in the phallic stage may result in many kinds of problems in adulthood, including exhibitionism, narcissism, deviance, frigidity and an inability to form stable relationships.

Next comes the **latency stage** (6 years-puberty). It is a time of relative tranquility because sexual impulses remain **latent** until puberty. During this stage children are mostly preoccupied with school work and playing with same-sex peers.

The **genital stage** (puberty onwards) is the final stage in Freud's psychoanalytic theory. It's when sexuality reappears, but this time it is directed into more appropriate partners. The genital stage doesn't cause any fixation. Possible problems in this stage arise from unresolved conflicts in earlier stages.

Bandura's social cognitive theory (SCT) is based on the concept that human behaviour influences and is influenced by personal factors (knowledge, goals, attitudes, culture, etc.) and the environmental factors. He calls this interaction **reciprocal determinism**. Among these lie key constructs of SCT such as self-efficacy, expectations, observational learning, behavioural capability and reinforcement.

Self-efficacy is probably the single most important determinant of behaviour. It's people's belief in their abilities to perform a task or achieve a goal. Even if you have the abilities to perform a task (**behavioural capability**), if your self-efficacy is low, you are likely to fail. **Observational learning** is learning by watching other people and imitating their behaviour. The strength of observational learning depends on how much we are motivated to copy observed behaviour, how much attention we pay to it, how well we remember it at some later time, and how physically and/or intellectually able we are to replicate it. A key factor associated with observational learning is **vicarious reinforcement**. It occurs when we imitate those behaviours that bring rewards and avoid those that are punished.

Behaviour is also influenced by **expectations**. In Bandura's view, people behave in a certain way because they expect some results from that behaviour. Expectations are, in turn, influenced by past experiences, observing what happens to others, and emotional or physical response that results from the behaviour.

Psychoanalytic and social cognitive theory are concerned with different aspects of development. Psychoanalytic theory focuses on the impact of sexual drives on people and their constant struggle to control them. Social cognitive theory, in distinct contrast, revolves around the concept of a cognitive process that takes place in a social context.

Choose the correct option.

1. Barbara chews on the ends of pencils or pens when she studies. According to the psychoanalytic theory of Freud, she may be fixated in the ________.
   a) oral stage   c) phallic stage
   b) anal stage   d) latency stage

2. A young man was arrested for exposing himself in a public park. According to Freud, the man's deviant behaviour was caused by fixation in ________.
   a) genital stage   c) oral stage
   b) phallic stage   d) anal stage

3. 5-year-old Donnie often tells his mother that he wants to marry her. Freud would conclude that the boy's behaviour is reflecting ________ .

   a) Oedipal complex c) genital complex
   b) Electra complex d) phallic complex

4. You are not likely to drink much in a social situation because you fear it will make you do stupid things. The belief you have about the consequences of drinking is called ________ .

   a) reciprocal determinism c) observational learning
   b) high self-efficacy d) outcome expectation

5. A shy child at school notices that another student is praised by the teacher for asking questions. The shy child wants to be praised too therefore he begins asking questions in the future. The shy student is exhibiting learning through ________ .

   a) behavioural capability c) vicarious reinforcement
   b) self-efficacy d) reciprocal determinism

6. Jack has applied for a job as a police officer and has been invited to an interview next Monday. Jack is confident about his abilities and believes and that the interview will go well. Jack most likely has ________ .

   a) behavioural capabilities c) an expectancy of reciprocal determinism
   b) high self-efficacy d) high outcome expectations

7. Andrew is unhappy in his job in a bank but he decides not to leave it for fear of not finding another one. This makes him dislike his job and neglect his duties. His superior notices his poor performance and in return starts to treat him worse than before. The way the superior treats Andrew is just a reaction to Andrew's attitude to his job and as such is an example of ________.

   a) vicarious reinforcement c) reciprocal determinism
   b) observational learning d) self-efficacy

8. The blue dress that Princess Kate wore at her engagement announcement to Prince William sold out in stores overnight as many people wanted to

copy that look. Copying someone's style of dressing is an example of ________ .

a) observational learning c) emotional response
b) reciprocal determinism d) vicarious reinforcement

Exercise 2

Read sentences a–g. Which personality component (*the id*, *the ego* or *the superego*) does 'it' in bold refer to? Replace 'it' with the appropriate component and then rearrange the sentences into a meaningful paragraph by numbering them from 1 to 6. Sentence c is the last sentence after rearrangement.

	a

It is the personality's moralist and judge. **It** tells us how to behave and punishes us for not meeting its demands with feelings of guilt and shame.

	b

It operates on the pleasure principle and it seeks immediate pleasure at any cost. **It** wants to eat, drink, get warm or get to sleep immediately. If these needs are not satisfied quickly, a person becomes anxious or tense.

7	c

The conflict between **it** and **it** takes place outside of conscious awareness, yet it affects human behaviour. Glimpses of the conflict can be occasionally seen in slips of the tongue or in dreams.

	d

It works on the reality principle, which means that it gratifies **it** in such a way that is socially and morally acceptable.

	e

The understanding that immediate pleasure is not always possible comes with development of a new structure of personality – **it**. **It** also seeks to satisfy pleasures and avoids pain, but it's realistic.

	f

However, life doesn't always work like that and the immediate gratification is not always realistic or even possible. Sometimes we need to wait until the right moment comes or until we develop a strategy or a plan to obtain pleasure.

	g

We are all born with **it**. **It** is an animal part of the self and is made of instinctive and primitive behaviours.

Exercise 3

Complete the sentences with the words from the box. Use the plural form if necessary.

trait, temperament, stereotype, type, fluid

The Theory of the Four Humours

One of the earliest theories of personalities was biological. The ancient Greek physician Hippocrates believed that a person's __________ (1) resulted from the balance of four __________ (2) (or what he called 'humours') within the body. The four humours were blood, yellow bile, black bile, and phlegm.

Galen, another Greek physician, extended the theory by proposing that the predominance of one or another of the four humours gave rise to four different personality __________ (3): sanguine (warm, optimistic, jolly, good-natured), melancholic (pessimistic, serious, introverted, depressed), choleric (hot-tempered, impulsive, restless), and phlegmatic (calm, aloof, thoughtful, patient).

The theory of the four humours was remarkably long-lasting. It was abandoned only in the mid-19th century following the rapid development of physiology. Although it's no longer taken seriously, the theory has encouraged many theorists to classify personality into various types or categories. In this respect, the humoural theory is said to be a precursor to __________ (4)-based theories. The most simplistic and oversimplified classification is based on __________ (5). For instance, we assume that a fat man will be jovial and a tall athletic man aggressive.

Exercise 4

Choose the correct option in italics in each of these sentences.

1. Personality is a set of *trails/traits* that are relatively consistent for an individual throughout his or her life span.
2. If a child becomes *fixated/fixed* at a particular stage, he or she will continue to be preoccupied with the *erogenous/erotic* zone associated with that stage.
3. During the latency stage, a child's sexual instincts are *late/latent*, which means that they temporarily repressed.
4. The id *seeks/slips* to satisfy its needs and urges immediately, even though the realities of life or rules of any kind dictate otherwise.
5. The ego tries to find realistic and appropriate ways of *gratifying/granting* the primitive impulses of the id.
6. Repressed sexual impulses and uncomfortable feelings rise occasionally to the surface of consciousness in *sleeps/slips* of the tongue and dreams.
7. According to Bandura, people with high *self-esteem/self-efficacy* set themselves challenging goals and are fully committed to meeting those goals.
8. Freud believed that all thoughts, feelings and behaviours are deeply affected by biological *drivings/drives* that are mostly unconscious.

9.

DEFENCE MECHANISMS

Exercise 1

Choose the correct option(s). More than one option is possible.

The concept of ego defence mechanisms is of particular importance in Sigmund Freud's personality theory. Defence mechanisms are unconscious psychological *states/devices/techniques* (1) that the ego uses to defuse the anxiety that arises when the *id's/ego's/superego's* (2) unacceptable urges come into conflict with the *id's/ego's/superego's* (3) demands to deny them. In doing so, the ego protects itself from unpleasant feelings, such as guilt or shame, and maintains a positive self-image.

The ego has developed a wide range of defence mechanisms, but not every single mechanism has been officially named yet. Psychologists have classified them according to how effective they are. Basically, the more mature a defence mechanism, the better it works. So instead of being pushed into the *unconsciousness/unconscious/subconscious* (4), undesired feelings and thoughts are transformed into less threatening forms.

Primitive/Immature/Simple (5) defences are quite effective in the short run and that's why they are favoured by children and those adults who happen not to know a better way of *dealing/managing/handling* (6) with their insecurities and fears. In the long run, however, they may *distort/obstruct/falsify* (7) reality and prevent insight into the true nature of the problem. Emotionally healthy adults usually use different strategies throughout their lives.

Exercise 2

Match the names of the defence mechanisms (1–10) with their definitions (a–j).

1. projection
2. rationalisation
3. repression
4. regression
5. denial
6. sublimation
7. displacement
8. reaction formation
9. isolation of affect
10. overcompensation

	a

Redirecting negative emotions (usually anger) from their original object to a substitute target in order to relieve tension.

	b

Retreating to an earlier stage of development rather than handling unpleasant situations in a mature manner.

	c

Behaving in a way that is exactly the opposite of one's true feelings.

	d

Detaching oneself from painful feelings or thoughts in order to avoid them.

	e

Attributing unacceptable thoughts or impulses to other people.

	f

Not accepting or acknowledging certain aspects of reality because it is too painful.

	g

Transforming unacceptable impulses into socially acceptable actions or behaviour.

	h

Pushing distressing feelings or thoughts into the unconscious.

	i

Making up for weaknesses or feelings of inadequacy in one area by excelling in other areas.

	j

Justifying controversial behaviour or feelings in a seemingly logical way to avoid uncomfortable emotions.

Exercise 3

Identify the defence mechanisms.

1. You convince yourself that you hate someone who you are really in love with because he/she doesn't reciprocate your affection.
2. Mike would like to go out on dates but he is too afraid of being turned down. Instead of plucking up the courage to ask a girl out, he says: 'I have no time for dating. I have to study to do well at school.'

3. When her boss told her to work over time Stacy didn't protest nor complain for fear of losing her job but when she came home, she shouted at her husband for not pulling his weight around the house.

4. A man whose marriage is at the verge of divorce talks about his marital problems in cold, rational terms without any emotions involved.

5. Even though Joe was arrested for drug possession, his parents refused to believe that he was an addict.

6. After hearing the bad news, Katy lay on the bed in a foetal position and started to suck her thumb. Then, she let herself have a good cry.

7. What Tim lacks in self-confidence due to his skinny build, he makes up for by yelling at his staff and generally being loud.

8. Alice is attracted to her male colleague but claims, without basis, that it is him who has sexual feelings about her.

9. A person who has violent tendencies that they don't wish to act upon, turn their aggressive energy into athletic activities.

10. The accuser said that he blocked out his memories of the abuse due to the trauma they caused. Little did he know that one day they would come flooding back to him.

Exercise 4

Choose the correct option in italics in each of these sentences.

1. Don't *repress/vent* your anger by driving in a way that is a menace to everyone.

2. Instead of *lashing/taking* out he turned his energy into physical exercise.

3. The man *blocked out/released* his memories of the war, but they reappeared after some time, triggered by a series of terrorist attacks.

4. Furious at his boss, Steve *displaced/redirected* his anger towards one of his co-workers.

5. He was unable to *deny/acknowledge* that he had a serious drink problem and was constantly saying that he might have had a shot or two of liquor every now and then.

6. By driving expensive cars, the man tried to *overcompensate/justify* for his small stature.

7. The boy *channelled/redirected* his violent tendencies into playing hockey.

8. Unable to cope with her loneliness, the girl *distanced/retreated* into a fantasy world, where her imaginary friends kept her company.

9. He wanted to *make/take* it up to his wife for whatever went wrong the previous night.

10. The student tried to *reason/justify* the failure to pass the exam by claiming that it was unfair.

11. It is you who are scared, not me. Don't *project/attribute* your fears onto me.

12. The ego may protect itself by *repressing/regressing* to an earlier stage of development.

13. The woman *distanced/retreated* herself from the painful emotions by standing back and focusing only on the facts.

Exercise 5

Complete the sentences with the verbs from the box in the right form.

negate, distort, operate, cope, reduce, relieve, substitute

1. People use multiple psychological strategies known as defence mechanisms to be able to maintain their self-esteem and __________ discomfort.

2. Defence mechanisms __________ on an unconscious level, which means that we are not aware of their use.

3. A person in denial __________ the harsh aspects of reality that produces too much stress for him to handle.

4. Defence mechanisms help us __________ negative thoughts and feelings to a manageable level.

5. The ego uses mature defence mechanism such as rationalisation to __________ with unpleasant reality instead of falsifying it.

6. Defence mechanisms may lead to maladaptive behaviours when an individual __________ them for more effective ways of dealing with difficult situations.

7. Primitive and less mature defence mechanisms effectively __________ reality, making it difficult or impossible for an individual to see his/her situation as it is.

10.

MENTAL ILLNESS

Exercise 1

You are most probably familiar with the words in italics. How about their meaning in the field of psychology?

performance, organic, disturb(ed), condition, substance

Now, read the text and do the exercise that follows.

A mental illness (also called mental disorder or psychopathology) is a health condition that disrupts the way we feel, think, and behave, impairing our social and occupational **performances**. Just like physical diseases, mental disorders can affect anyone, irrespective of age, gender, race, intellect, social class or income level, and can be managed with prevention, diagnosis, and specific treatment.

Mental illness has been known throughout the history and across cultures, and the way it was thought about was heavily influenced by societal views, superstitious beliefs and knowledge (or a lack of it). In antiquity, physicians and scientists (assuming that such a category existed) considered mental illness an **organic** problem and offered physiological explanations. For instance, Hippocrates thought that depression resulted from an excess of black bile. Yet there were vast majorities of people who believed that mental illness came from the gods and that the mentally ill were punished for their wrongdoings. Religious remedies were sought in the hope that the gods, if placated, could cure them of their madness. At the same time people with milder forms of abnormal behaviour were believed to be endowed by the gods with some special powers, for instance the power of predicting the future. In the Middle Ages, the mental illness was no longer seen as imbalances in the body, but it was thought to be caused by demonic possessions and exorcism was used as the treatment. Some cases of mental illness were also attributed to witchcraft. Since natural disasters such as plagues, crop failure or droughts weren't well understood at the time, witches' curses made an easy explanation. Witch-hunting began and a lot of mentally **disturbed** women were burned at the stake. These beliefs are probably responsible for the fear that mental illness still evokes in people.

The witch craze came to an end only in the 18th century, after an estimated 50,000 presumed witches were executed. When the Age of Enlightenment began to take hold, mental illness became increasingly accepted as a disease and mental institutions (called at the time 'lunatic asylums') were developed to remove the mentally ill from society and keep them out of harm's way. Yet, it was not until the 19th and 20th centuries that scientific methods were applied to the study and treatment of abnormal behaviour.

Psychiatry has come a long way since the days when mentally disturbed people were declared demon-possessed, locked up or burned at the stake, yet scientists still don't know the exact aetiology of mental disorders. It is generally believed, however, that mental disorders are a result of a combination of biological, psychological and social factors.

There are more than 200 classified forms of mental illness, including schizophrenia, anxiety disorders (a broad term for a range of anxiety **conditions** such as generalised anxiety disorder (GAD), obsessive-compulsive disorder (OCD), post-traumatic stress disorder (PTSD), panic disorder (PD) and phobic disorders), mood disorders (e.g. bipolar disorder and major depressive disorder), personality disorders (e.g. narcissistic personality disorder, antisocial personality disorder and borderline personality disorder), eating disorders (e.g. anorexia nervosa and bulimia nervosa), sleep disorders (e.g. insomnia and narcolepsy), **substance** use disorders (e.g. alcohol abuse) and dissociative disorders (e.g. dissociative fugue and conversion disorder). With 13% of the global burden of disease, they are a major public health issue, surpassing cancer, cardiovascular disease and diabetes.

Decide if the following statements are true (T) or false (F).

1. Mental disorders require medical approaches that are comparable to those applied to physical diseases.
2. It was a prevailing view in the Middle Ages that abnormal behaviour was brought about by evil spirits.
3. In the 18th century, most people kept perceiving the mentally ill as demon-possessed and locked them up in mental asylums.
4. 13% of people worldwide suffer from mental disorders.
5. More people suffer from mental disorders than from cancer, cardiovascular disease and diabetes taken together.
6. There are a variety of anxiety disorders.

Exercise 2

a) Match words from box A and B to make the names of symptoms of mental disorders, e.g. ***excessive worry.***

A

~~excessive~~, auditory, emotional, restrictive, ritualistic, partial, pounding, suicidal, intrusive, mood

B

eating, paralysis, thoughts (×2), hallucinations, ~~worry~~, swings, behaviours, numbness, heart

b) Complete the texts with the symptoms from Exercise 3a. What disorders do these people most likely suffer from?

1.

I've always been a worrywart, but my worrying nature never interfered with my daily life until quite recently when I've got carried away worrying too much about almost everything. Even the thought of getting through the day can be overwhelming and debilitating. Because of my __________ I can't sleep well at night so during the day I'm totally drained and I can't focus at work.

2.

Christie was a chubby and happy child but her happiness ended when she started school. Her classmates taunted her, calling her 'fat' and 'ugly' just about every day. She became self-conscious almost overnight but it wasn't until her mid-teens when she decided to change her eating habits to lose weight. What started as a reasonable diet plan turned with time into __________ and persistent thoughts about weight. She wouldn't eat anything but low-calorie foods, such as rice cakes, and refused to admit that she had a problem.

3.

The first symptoms of Paul's disorder showed up when he was about 17 years old. At the time it was a paralysing fear of his house getting burgled or burnt down. He couldn't leave the house without making sure that the doors were locked and that the stove was turned off. Soon his condition spread to other areas and normal life became impossible. He involuntarily became engaged in __________ such as excessive hand washing or repeating a series of action several times. He even started to have __________ of harming others, which was totally out of character for him.

4.

Michael has been suffering from this disorder most of his adult life, however his problems didn't surface until he finished college and got a job in a secondary school library. One day he began to have __________ with voices threatening him and commenting on his actions. Subsequently he became suspicious that his boss wanted to poison him. At first his colleagues were unaware of Michael's condition, but when he started talking 'in a weird way' and mumbling to himself, they became alarmed and called his parents to voice their concerns.

5.
I have been suffering from severe __________ for some time now. They can send me into a manic frenzy that makes me energetic and disinhibited to the extreme, and then sink me into a depression pit deeper than most people will ever realise. When I'm there I don't feel like getting out of bed and facing the day. I don't understand why I feel this way, but I've reached the point where I get __________. On one occasion I tried to cut my wrists with a razor blade, but at the last moment I lost my resolve. Now my disorder is in remission and I'm doing really well.

6.
Susanna is in her mid-20s and suffers from some kind of disorder. Generally, she feels highly uncomfortable and nervous in front of other people. In those situations she has an excessive fear that she's being watched and that she will embarrass herself. All of a sudden she gets a __________ that feels like it's going to beat out of her chest and she breaks out in a sweat. Since meeting people has become Susanna's worst nightmare, she goes to great lengths to avoid any social events or gatherings. She can't even go out with her good friends without having a drink or two. Deep down she knows that her fears are unreasonable, but she is unable to overcome them.

7.
Adam was involved in a serious car accident. He emerged unscathed from it, unlike his wife who was killed on the spot. A few days later, Adam woke up unable to move his legs. His parents took him to hospital, but the doctors couldn't initially explain his __________ and found no evidence of injury to his body or infection. After a comprehensive review of his condition, he was told that his immobility is psychosomatic, not physical.

8.
After returning home from the war in Syria, John is not able to get his life back on track. Unlike many other soldiers, he came through the war without any lasting physical damage, yet he is haunted with distressing flashbacks of his military service. As a result, he is struggling with __________, anxiety and poor sleep. His wife tries to get him to see a therapist, but he refuses to go, saying that he doesn't have any problems.

c) In the texts, find synonyms to:

1. period of recovery
2. craze
3. acute
4. somatic
5. recurrent recollections

Exercise 3

Choose the correct option in italics in each of these sentences.

1. Due to alcohol poisoning, the man suffered from *paranoid/paranoia* delusions that he was a victim of political conspiracy. Moreover, he developed *blurred/slurred* speech, which made him hard to understand.

2. If an individual experiences *gustatory/olfactory* hallucinations, his/her food may taste as if it was bad, rotten or poisoned.

3. Social *withdrawal/retreat* is basically avoiding people and social situations. It's not limited only to social phobia. It's also associated with other mental illnesses, such as depression, schizophrenia or eating disorders.

4. I couldn't concentrate or think straight with my *running/racing* thoughts. Trying to keep up with them made me feel exhausted and I thought that my head was going to explode.

5. A: 'All of a sudden I have the feeling of intense heat which spreads throughout my whole body and I feel like someone has turned on an oven inside me.'

   B: 'It must be those hot *blushes/flashes*!'

6. Dorothy is struggling with bouts of *low/down* mood and lethargy, which she initially attributed to stress in her workplace. She has a stream of

negative thoughts that leave her feeling worthless and undeserving of anything good in life.

7. The patient often displays *erratic/erroneous* behaviours as a result of his varying moods. One minute he is chatting happily and smiling, and the next he is the exact opposite.

8. Narcissists have a *grandeur/grandiose* sense of self-importance and a strong need for admiration. That is why they exaggerate their achievements and abilities, even if objectively they are just ordinary.

9. Patients suffering from thought *insertion/injection* repeatedly complain of having thoughts put into their minds by external forces.

10. In addition to feeling restless, people with GAD are very likely to experience dry *lips/mouth*. If this occurs, the person affected needs to sip drink while eating or talking, even when he/she is not really thirsty.

11. Oblivious to everyone around, Melanie stared at a point outside the window in a catatonic *stupor/sopor*.

12. Schizophrenic patients speaking 'word *salad/stew*' use a mixture of meaningless and unrelated words that are incomprehensible to their listeners and often to themselves as well.

Exercise 4

Complete the sentences below with the right preposition.

1. Hormonal fluctuations put women more ______ risk for anxiety disorders than men.

2. It's believed that genetic factors predispose people ______ anxiety disorders.

3. A stressful event is a major catalyst ______ anxiety.

4. People affected ______ obsessive-compulsive disorder suffer ______ intrusive thoughts that disturb their everyday lives.

5. Sleep disorders such as narcolepsy or insomnia involve disruption caused ______ normal sleep patterns.

6. People who are diagnosed ______ panic disorder often go ______ episodes of irrational, intense fear.

7. Although anxiety disorders are treatable ______ psychotherapy and medication, a lot of people ______ anxiety don't seek help.

8. A large number of mentally ill patients respond very well ______ therapy, thanks to which they can live fulfilling lives.

9. Sufferers of bipolar personality disorder are prone ______ aggressive, impulsive acts.

10. There are higher rates ______ women for some mental illnesses such as eating disorders and anxiety disorders, whilst men are more vulnerable ______ antisocial personality disorders.

Exercise 5

Complete the sentences with the verbs from the box in the right form.

strike, disrupt, relapse, mimic, affect, overlap, trigger, exacerbate

1. Mental disorders come in different forms, with each form __________ an individual's life in different ways.

2. For people with Generalized Anxiety Disorder, stress is a factor that __________ their condition.

3. Although mental illnesses __________ millions of people worldwide, they are still feared and stigmatised.

4. Many anxiety disorders ___________ to a large degree. It is not unusual for an individual suffering from GAD to experience also panic attacks.

5. If a panic attack ___________ you while you are riding in a lift, you may later develop a phobia of lifts or any other enclosed space.

6. Almost all people suffering from anxiety disorders believe that their symptoms are physical since anxiety attacks can ___________ physical disorders such as heart disease or asthma.

7. Seeing people dressed in black ___________ anxiety in some people.

8. When the patient discontinued his medication, his illness quickly ___________.

Exercise 6

a) Study the meaning of the prefixes and complete the third column of the table with the opposites of the words in italics. There may be more than one answer for some words.

diagnose, sane, function, predictable, adaptive, regard, inhibited, ability, normal, balance, curable, use, formed, legal, rational, nourished, trustful, psychotic, responsible, stability, depressant, mobility, stable, coherent, able, anxiety

Prefix	Meaning	Example Words
ab	away from, outside of	abuse
anti	against	antisocial
dis	the opposite of something	disincentive
dys	difficult, not normal	dysregulation
il	not, before ‚l'	illogical

im	not, before ‚b', ‚m' and ‚p'	immoral
in	not	inadequate
ir	not, before ‚r'	irrecoverable
mal	badly, wrongly	maltreat
mis	bad, badly, wrongly	mistreat
un	not	unconscious

b) Complete the sentences with the words from the table.

1. Some individuals ___________ alcohol in order to find relief from a psychological problem, such as depression or anxiety.
2. Approximately one in three people will experience a form of ___________ behaviour at some point in their lives.
3. Borderline personality disorder is a condition characterised by ___________ of behaviours and interpersonal relationships.
4. The patient rarely spoke, and when he did his statements were ___________ and full of words that no one could understand.
5. Many people with anxiety disorders experience significant problems with obsessive and ___________ thoughts.
6. Borderline personality disorder and bipolar disorder are both marked by ___________ moods and therefore can be ___________ as each other.
7. An individual falls into ___________ behaviours so as not to face or resolve anxiety. Not only these behaviours don't help, but also create additional problems over time. A common example is substance abuse.
8. Recent research in neuroscience corroborates the theory that mental disorders are caused by ___________ of the brain.

9. The condition of the patient with conversion disorder has progressively deteriorated to complete __________ so she has to use a wheelchair now.

10. Individuals with antisocial personality disorder may seem gentle and charming, but it's all an act. In reality they have diminished empathy and show a complete __________ for social norms.

11. The reason why some mentally disturbed people refuse to seek help is that they're afraid of social stigma of being labelled '__________' and 'dangerous'.

12. The girl restricted her diet so much that within a few weeks she became __________ and had to be hospitalised.

NOTE

If an illness has been **misdiagnosed** it means that it has not been diagnosed correctly, whereas if an illness has been **undiagnosed** it means that it has not been identified or diagnosed.

Some noun/adjective pairs take different prefixes to form the opposites, e.g.

instability but **unstable**, **inability** but **unable**.

Exercise 7

Match the drug class with the drug action.

1. antialcoholics
2. antidepressants
3. antipsychotics (or neuroleptics)
4. anxiolytics
5. hypnotics
6. mood stabilisers
7. sedatives (or tranquilisers)

8. stimulants

   a) induce sleep
   b) relieve anxiety symptoms
   c) help to calm and relax
   d) suppress mood swings between mania and depression
   e) relieve depression symptoms
   f) relieve psychotic symptoms (e.g. hallucinations and delusions)
   g) increases alertness and awareness
   h) reduce the cravings for alcohol

11.

ADDICTION

Exercise 1

Read the text and choose the right answer.

Addiction is characterised by a compulsive and repetitive use of a mind-altering substance or behaviour despite severe negative health, social and legal consequences. An individual develops a ___________ (1) by engaging in ___________ (2) behaviours, which means that instead of meeting their lives' challenges, they turn to alcohol or drugs in an attempt to ease their plight. At first, these substances appear to provide a ___________ (3), but nothing further. Actually they only make things worse. Addictive substance activates the reward circuitry of the brain, producing the 'high' that the brain learns to look forward to. Over time, a user's reaction to a substance decreases so that a larger dose has to be taken to achieve the initial thrill. This is how ___________ (4) develops and any attempt to abruptly cease what the individual is taking or using may lead to ___________ (5) symptoms.

When people talk about addiction, what they think of right away is drug abuse and alcohol abuse, but it doesn't necessarily have to involve substance dependence. Many addiction professionals agree that addiction may include virtually anything from gambling and playing video games to seemingly ___________ (6) activities such as shopping, eating, exercising and working. In other words, addiction may refer to substance addiction (e.g. drug abuse) or behavioural addiction (e.g. compulsive shopping). Although substance addiction and behavioural addiction have some similarities (such as ___________ (7), compulsion, and continued use even in face of harmful effects), there's a major difference between them. Whereas substance abuse __________ (8) brain function and causes physiological and psychological harm to the user, behavioural addictions result only in psychological and social consequences.

A prevailing view of addiction is that addicts cannot successfully __________ (9) on their own, however many studies (including the one on Vietnam War veterans) show that it's possible to __________ (10) addiction without professional treatment. They are in no way suggesting, however, that therapy isn't good or that everyone is expected to cure themselves. The bottom line is that if addicts don't help themselves or don't allow other people to help them, the situation becomes increasingly difficult. They don't only ruin their own lives, they take their families down with them in the process.

1. a) habit	b) dependency	c) ritual
2. a) maladaptive	b) deviant	c) dysfunctional
3. a) relieve	b) respite	c) reprieve
4. a) resistance	b) tolerance	c) habituation
5. a) abstinence	b) withdrawal	c) prohibition
6. a) harmful	b) malignant	c) innocuous
7. a) craving	b) hunger	c) urge
8. a) influences	b) impairs	c) afflicts
9. a) regress	b) relapse	c) recover
10. a) ease	b) break	c) free

Exercise 2

Two of the three options are correct. Which one is incorrect?

1. Physical dependence occurs when people's bodies become *accustomed/dependent/addicted* to a substance.

2. Most people start *taking/doing/making* drugs voluntarily.

3. Alcohol and drug abuse are easily recognisable *self-destructive/compulsive/addicted* behaviours.
4. Drinking too much coffee is a(n) *practice/bad habit/addiction* I picked up in college.
5. Addictions involve *excessive/often/repetitive* use of pleasurable activities to handle life's challenges.
6. 'Soft addictions' are those seemingly *bad/harmless/benign* activities such as compulsive texting or shopping.
7. Genetics, alongside environmental factors, can affect a person's *sensitivity/susceptibility/predisposition* to a drug.
8. Generally, women are more likely to *abstain/restrain/refrain* from drinking alcohol than men.
9. Some people can drink for years without becoming addicted, whereas others quickly fall *loss/victim/prey* to addiction.
10. It is not uncommon for drug addicts to steal to *feed/kick/support* their bad habit.

Exercise 3

Replace the colloquial italicised parts of the sentences with more formal equivalents from the box in the right form.

intoxicated by, be inebriated, start drinking, smoke, be dependent, relapse, take an overdose, become addicted to, quit abruptly, reduce, quit, crave

1. After losing his job, John *turned to the bottle.*
2. I'm finally off drugs. I no longer *have that monkey on my back*.
3. He *fell off the wagon* after two years of sobriety.

4. Alison *got hooked on* nicotine when she was 15 when her friend offered her a cigarette.
5. Paul is an alcoholic, but he wants to *kick the habit* for the sake of his family.
6. A: 'Are you still smoking?'

   B: 'No, my doctor diagnosed me with asthma so I *went cold turkey.*'
7. *Cutting down on* caffeine may help you improve your sleep pattern.
8. A: 'Are you sure she *OD'd*?'

   B: 'Yes, the blood tests came back positive.'
9. Whenever she was *jonesing for* a cigarette, she started to chew a nicotine gum.
10. Most people at the party were *doped up on* booze.
11. The man kept drinking until he *went out of his skull*.
12. He's a heroin addict. He started out *chasing the dragon* but soon moved to using needles.

NOTE

Both **jones** and **crave** are used in reference to food or addictive substances.

Jones is usually put in the continuous form e.g. 'I'm jonesing for a smoke', and **crave** is usually put in the simple form, e.g. 'I crave a smoke right now.'

Craving is the feeling you get from an addiction or a strong desire. Unlike **crave**, **craving** takes the preposition 'for', e.g. 'I have a craving for a chocolate.'

Exercise 4

Match the routes of administration in column A with the names of substances in column B.

A	B
1. ingestion	a) cocaine
2. inhalation	b) stimulants and depressants

3. injection c) marijuana, crack cocaine, nicotine
4. snorting/snuffing d) heroin

Exercise 5

Complete the sentences with the words from the box. Use the plural form if necessary.

compulsive hoarder, alcohol abuser, caffeine addict, workaholic, webaholic, compulsive eater, heavy smoker, compulsive shopper, drug addict, gambler

1. Like many other ___________, Scott has lost lots of money in casinos and run up huge debts. Despite this, he continues to play desperately hoping that his bad luck will end eventually.
2. The stereotype of a(n) ___________ portrays a person who drinks to ease his or her psychological pain.
3. My boss is a(n) ___________. He puts his work above everything else and never has time to take a break. He may lose his marriage if he doesn't reevaluate his priorities.
4. Ellen always seems to be on a diet. It's hard to believe that she used to be a(n) ___________ in her late teens.
5. My sister is a(n) ___________ but she tries to quit the habit by wearing nicotine patches and chewing gum.
6. Betty is a(n) ___________. She can spend, not just hours, but days in shopping centres buying things half of which she can hardly afford.
7. Many people hang on to treasures from the past and yet their houses do not, even remotely, resemble the houses of ___________, which are cluttered to the point of being uninhabitable by any social standards.
8. He used to be a(n) ___________, doing heroin and meth, but he man-

aged to turn his life around with the help of a rehab facility and a desire for abstinence.

9. Back in my college days I drank four or more coffees a day. I also drank coffee in the evenings when I needed to stay up to study before tests and exams. Thankfully I'm no longer a(n) __________.

10. I'm fairly positive Tom is a(n) __________. He seems to be as hooked on the Net as other people are on nicotine or drugs.

Exercise 6

Replace the italicised withdrawal symptoms/signs with their equivalents in the box.

myalgia, lacrimation, nausea, diarrhoea, rhinorrhea, pupillary dilation, hyperalgesia, abdominal cramping

A 38-year-old man presented to the A&E department (Accident and Emergency) of his local hospital complaining of *feeling sick* (1), *frequent watery stools* (2) *increased tearing* (3) as well as *muscle aches* (4). On admittance, he had *enlarged pupils* (5), a fever of 39°C, and a high blood pressure. He explained that he had 'some difficulties with drug use' and a subsequent examination revealed that he'd been regularly taking opiates (including heroin and morphine) but stopped using them to get his life back. He was also suffering from *stomach aches* (6), *increased sensitivity to pain* (7) and a *runny nose* (8). The man was given loperamide, meclizine and ibuprofen for diarrhoea, nausea and pain relief, respectively. He was also administered naloxone, which resulted in a reversal of the symptoms in a relatively short time.

When the man's condition got better, he was referred to an intensive outpatient treatment program (IOP), where he continued to get help needed to break his addiction.

12. HUMAN DEVELOPMENT

Exercise 1

Read the text and do the exercise that follows.

Human life begins when the fertilised egg (**zygote**) begins to *divide* through the process of **cell division** known as **mitosis**. One cell becomes two, two becomes four, and so forth, doubling each time. When the zygote has about 150 cells, it *implants* itself in the wall of the **uterus**. At this stage, it becomes an **embryo**. It is when that most internal and external organs start to form, including the brain, the heart, the stomach, eyes are ears. Some cells split away and turn into a disc-shaped organ called the **placenta**. The placenta is attached to the embryo through the **umbilical cord**. Over the course of gestation, the placenta provides the developing baby with oxygen and nutrients, and *discharges* its waste into the mother's blood. The embryo itself *floats* in a watery sac called the **amniotic sac**. The sack is filled with **amniotic fluid**, which helps to protect the embryo from bumps and changes in temperature.

From the end of the eighth week until the time of **delivery**, the embryo is called a **foetus**, which in Latin means 'hatching of young'. As the **gestation** progresses, the foetus assumes an increasingly human form and its organs further *develop* and *mature*.

At 21 weeks of gestation, the foetus is able to *discern* a variety of flavours using its senses of smell and taste. It can hear sounds from outside the **womb** by the 27 week. **Pupillary response** to light develops around 29 weeks and is usually present by 31 or 32 weeks. At 32 weeks of gestation, the foetus consistently responds to temperature, pressure or pain, and touch is what allows to experience these sensations. Under normal circumstances, with the exception of sight, babies come to the world with quite well-developed senses.

Prenatal sensory experiences bias newborns' behaviours and preferences. For one thing, they suck longer when they are exposed to sweet-tasting food and *recoil* from unpleasant odours, such as rotten eggs. For another, they prefer their mothers' voices over any other sound. Newborns can also make out lights of different brightness, shapes and movement, however their **distance vision** is poor. They can best see objects that are 20 to 30 cm away, and anything further is unclear. Handily, this **nearsightedness** makes newborns prefer human faces to other visual stimuli. No wonder that at this age, they have a particular interest in the face and voice of their mothers. By the time babies are three months, they can perceive depth. In fact, many advances in **vision development** take place at 2 and 3 months of age. Babies' **visual acuity** becomes sharper, their eyes move better and they learn to *switch* their gaze from one object to another without moving their heads. Around this time, infants already show fairly advanced abilities to interpret complex sensory information and are well on their way to reach the adult level of visual abilities.

Newborns arrive in the world also with a set of **simple reflexes** – automatic, involuntary responses to certain stimuli – that helps them survive in the new environment. Examples include the sucking reflex, the rooting reflex, and the Moro reflex. Most of the reflexes begin to disappear by the second month, with a majority of them gone by the fourth month. There are other forms of reflexes, however, that are not present at birth and generally appear after two months. These are **postural reflexes** and they include body righting, neck righting and parachute reflexes. They vanish around the first year of life and are replaced by more voluntary movement behaviours.

In the first year of life, babies go through a period of rapid growth. As they develop physically, their muscle control increases and locomotor skills improve. **Locomotor development** proceeds from general to specific movements and from the head to the legs. At some point, babies can hold up their head, then chest, then they can sit, crawl and after that stand, and eventually walk. By 15 months most babies can walk around by themselves.

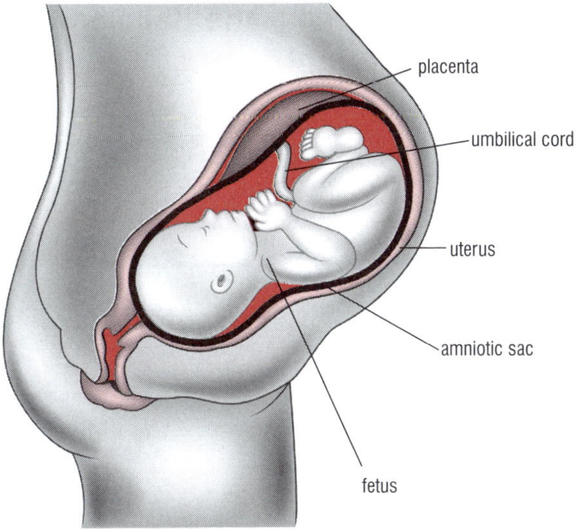

Decide if the following sentences are true (T) or false (F).

1. From eight and forty weeks, the developing organism is called a baby.
2. Babies' sensory experiences start long before they are born.
3. The placenta provides a constant temperature around the developing baby.
4. The foetus receives a large amount of sensory information through tactile perception.
5. Infants have blurry vision at birth.
6. Gustatory and olfactory responses are not present by 22 weeks of gestation.
7. Newborns have an innate preference for sweet tastes.
8. Locomotor development occurs from the legs upwards.

Exercise 2

Complete the sentences with the italicised verbs from the text in Exercise 1 in the right form.

1. After the egg is ___________, it undergoes a series of cell divisions, known as mitosis.
2. Soon after conception, the zygote ___________ itself in the uterus.
3. The zygote ___________ into an embryo, then into a foetus and then into a child.
4. The placenta ___________ the wastes of the developing baby into the maternal circulatory system.
5. As it ___________ in the amniotic fluid, the foetus is protected from blows to the mother's abdomen.
6. By 4 weeks nearly all of the baby's major organs are beginning to ___________.
7. Already at 21 weeks, the foetus can ___________ different flavours.
8. Newborn babies typically move their heads while ___________ their gaze from one point to another.

Exercise 3

a) **Complete the table with the correct forms of the missing parts of speech.**

Noun	Adjective
uterus	
placenta	

	amniotic
	umbilical
foetus	
embryo	
	pupillary
reflex	

b) Complete the sentences with the words from the table.

1. The __________ develops into a fluid-filled sac, which provides a safe environment for the unborn child.
2. Even though the baby is moving constantly inside the womb, the mother may not be able to feel the __________ movements until 16 to 25 weeks.
3. Much of the newborn's behaviours are __________. For example, when you put an infant into water, they would hold their breath and move their arms and legs.
4. The __________ is the scar on the abdomen that remains after the umbilical cord is cut at birth.
5. Labour begins with __________ contractions, usually after nine months of gestation.
6. The remarkable ability of __________ stem cells to grow into almost any cell type in the body could be used in transplantation medicine.
7. Some toxic substances, including alcohol and drugs, can cross the __________ barrier and damage the developing organism.
8. If light enters the eyes, the __________ will constrict in response.

Exercise 4

Choose the correct option.

Piaget's Theory of Cognitive Development

Before Jean Piaget, a Swiss developmental psychologist and philosopher, most theorists believed that children are how they are because they are less intelligent than adults. Piaget questioned this assumption and showed that it was not a matter of intelligence; it was just that children think in fundamentally different ways compared to adults. According to Piaget children are active thinkers or little scientists who are constantly __________ (1) their environment and __________ (2) their knowledge by means of experience and according to their age. They do so eagerly and naturally because they are __________ (3) motivated and don't need rewards from adults to learn.

In Piaget's theory, learning occurs through two complementary processes: assimilation and accommodation. **Assimilation** involves __________ (4) new information into existing mental frameworks commonly known as **schemas**, whilst **accommodation** involves __________ (5) existing schemas or creating new ones to deal with the new information. When children can assimilate new information into existing schemas, they are said to be in a state of cognitive balance, called **equilibrium**. When something doesn't fit into existing schemas, a confusing state of **disequilibrium** occurs. Then children try to __________ (6) the balance through accommodation.

Piaget claimed that cognitive development is a systematic, structured process and all children go through four stages, __________ (7) from sensory reactions to logical and abstract thought: **sensorimotor** (infancy), **pre-operational** (early childhood), **concrete operational** (middle childhood/preadolescence) and **formal operational** (adolescence and adulthood) in sequence, however the rate at which they do so may vary. For instance, children from more supportive and stimulating environments __________ (8) the cognitive tasks of each stage faster than less privileged children.

Although most psychologists agree with Piaget's view of development, some point to its flaws. One of the objections refers to children's cognitive skills.

The critics believe that children are more intellectually able at each stage than Piaget suspected.

1. a) interacting	b) exploring	c) inventing
2. a) using	b) applying	c) accumulating
3. a) intrinsically	b) imminently	c) implicitly
4. a) adding	b) incorporating	c) attributing
5. a) replacing	b) matching	c) modifying
6. a) restore	b) challenge	c) strike
7. a) progressing	b) starting	c) continuing
8. a) develop	b) master	c) resolve

Exercise 5

Complete the sentences below with the verbs from the box in the right form.

reason, organise, reverse, construct, acquire, conserve, experience, cease

1. Pre-operational children cannot __________ a sequence of events. For instance, they can take apart a jigsaw puzzle, but are unable to put it back together.

2. A baby as young as 6 months believes that if an object is removed from his/her sight, it __________ to exist.

3. Children __________ knowledge through testing their ideas and learning from the results.

4. Infants cannot __________ yet. They __________ the environment around them only through their senses and motor skills.

5. Due to their limitations in thinking, preschoolers __________ a totally different interpretation of the world than adults.

6. Children ___________ their knowledge of the world into schemas, which become more complex and nuanced over time.

7. In the preoperational stage the child doesn't yet have the ability to ___________, so he/she believes that, for example, pouring a glass of water into a taller but narrower glass changes its amount.

Exercise 6

a) Analyse the answers/reactions to the questions and then match them to the concepts derived from Piaget's theory of cognitive development.

Questions	Answers/Reactions
1. Why does the sun shine?	To make me warm.
2. What are the clouds?	The smoke from daddy's pipe.
3. Why does the sun hide behind the clouds?	Because it's sad.
4. Where is the ball? (you ask a baby after you've hidden the ball under the table)	The baby loses an interest in the ball.
5. Where is more play dough? (you ask a child after you've made two balls of play dough and rolled out one of them)	The child points at the rolled out play dough.

a) **animistic thinking** (**animism**) – children's belief that inanimate objects have human qualities (e.g. feelings and emotions)

b) **artificialism** – children's assumption that everything in nature is made by human beings

c) **egocentrism** – children's tendency to view the world from their own point of view

d) no **conservation** – children's inability to understand that the basic properties of a substance (number, mass, volume) are unaffected by certain transformations that change their appearance

e) no **object permanence** – children's inability to understand that objects continue to exist even though they are removed from sight

Exercise 7

a) Read the text and then replace the underlined words with the ones from the box in the right form.

utterance, imitate, mastery, combine, absorb, hard-wired, utter

Language Acquisition

No discussion about a child's cognitive development would be complete without taking into account the development of language. The way children come to know their native language has been the subject of lengthy – and sometimes heated – debate among linguists, psychologists, philosophers and other scholars. One of the earliest scientific explanations of language development was proposed by B.F. Skinner, who believed that language is a behaviour and, like any other cognitive behaviour, it must be learnt. He argued that children learn language through <u>mimicking</u> (1) adults who reward correct <u>sentences</u> (2) and discourage incorrect ones on the basis of operant conditioning principles. As a result, the meaningful words and phrases are remembered and used in the future and the nonsense words are forgotten. A very different view was provided by Noam Chomsky. He pointed out that language is way too complex to be acquired through operant conditioning alone. Chomsky's belief was that children are born with a **language acquisition device** (LAD), which allows them to learn the language they hear around them naturally. Eric Lenneberg added his own twist to the theory. He agreed that children are born with the ability to learn language, but he said that there is a critical period for doing so. If language acquisition doesn't occur by **puberty**, a child will never achieve a <u>full command</u> (3) of language.

By contrast, Piaget believed that there's no inborn (4) language device in the brain. Instead, language is part of general cognitive development and as such its acquisition follows the stages of cognitive development.

Although babies can't speak at birth, language learning begins before they are born. In the uterus they are exposed to a variety of sounds including their mothers' voice. It's in the uterus where they learn some **characteristics** of the language, therefore babies just 4 days out of the womb are able to distinguish one language from another. Around 6 weeks of age, they start **cooing** when they feel good and from about 16 weeks they start laughing. At some point between 4 and 6 months of age, most babies begin to **babble**. Early babbling consists of strings of **consonants** and **vowels** such as 'ba-ba' or 'goo-goo.' Gradually it develops into more complex combinations of sounds, e.g. 'bagidabu.' By 9 or 10 months, babbling begins to sound more and more like real **speech**. From there it's not long before children say (5) their first single words. This usually happens somewhere around their first birthday. The first words are often accompanied by **gestures** and **facial expressions**, which help babies indicate their wants. By about 18 months, most children start putting (6) two words together in simple, laconic sentences, such as 'doggy here' or 'Mommy go.' At that point, children's vocabulary starts **expanding** at a rapid pace. Thus, at 2 typically developing children know about 200 words, which builds to approximately 1,000 words at around 3 years of age and to several thousand by age 6 or so. Usually by the end of their third year, most acquire the basic rules for **forming** plurals and the past tense, and start using function words such as 'and', 'some' or 'would.' Over the next few years, children's vocabulary **grows** even more and so does grammar. Whilst grammatical development goes on throughout childhood, language development never ends. Even adults are still taking in (7) new words.

b) Decide if the following sentences are true (T) or false (F).

1. B.F. Skinner argued that speaking was a learnt behaviour.

2. According to Noam Chomsky, babies are predisposed to language.

3. Humans are born with the ability to recognise familiar sounds.

4. Babbling is a baby's first true words.

5. Babies typically use gestures by the average age of 5 months.

6. A typical 18-month-old child can't yet produce a concise sentence.

7. Vocabulary acquisition accelerates around the age of 1.

8. The process of expanding one's vocabulary never ends.

c) What do the following terms refer to in the text?

- the critical period hypothesis
- holophrases
- telegraphic speech
- vocabulary spurt

Exercise 8

a) Match the beginnings in column A to the endings in column B to make correct expressions.

A	B
1. put	a) 200 words
2. expand	b) gestures and vocalisations
3. accumulate	c) one's thoughts
4. speak in	d) one's repertoire of words
5. detect	e) language skills
6. use	g) two words together
7. develop	h) complete sentences
8. communicate	i) differences in word order

b) Complete the sentences below using the expressions from Exercise 2 in the right form.

1. It's not uncommon for parents to worry that their two-year-olds can't ____________________. Some toddlers don't even talk until they are 3.

2. By as early as 18 months of age, babies ____________________ at a very rapid pace.

3. Around the age of 2, the average child ____________________ and starts producing two-word utterances, such as 'Mummy come.'

4. By their third birthday, children start ____________, though simple, ____________.

5. Children are able to ____________________ way before they produce grammatical sentences themselves and most know that 'Big Bird is tickling Cookie Monster' means something different from 'Cookie Monster is tickling Big Bird.'

6. Babies ____________________ prior to using spoken language.

7. Children ____________________ through interactions with more advanced speakers of the language.

8. As children's vocabulary grows, they are able to ____________________ more accurately.

13.

SOCIAL PSYCHOLOGY

Exercise 1

Read the text and do the exercise that follows.

Social psychology studies how people's feelings, thoughts, attitudes and behaviours are influenced by other people and the social context in which they occur. It also studies how people collect, interpret and assess information of other people. The study of how people perceive and think about one another is called **social cognition** and is a major area of interest in social psychology.

Forming first **impressions** about people is a complex phenomenon. Generally, we form impressions about others using **preconceived ideas** based on past experience that help us categorise and define people. These preconceived ideas are called **schemas** or **schemata** (the concept of schema is introduced in chapter 6). For instance, if you see a man wearing blue scrubs and latex gloves, you may rightly categorise him as a surgeon. Closely connected with 'the surgeon' category is a schema of a certain set of beliefs and expectations. For most people, surgeons are respected, highly trained and qualified medical professionals who specialise in surgical procedures. This particular schema, in turn, influences how you perceive the man in scrubs and how you behave around him.

Generally, schemas help us quickly categorise people and respond appropriately to them, but not all schemas are helpful. Sometimes they are inaccurate and lead us to view other people in inappropriate ways. This is because our schemas are significantly influenced by the phenomenon known as the

primacy effect. Basically, it means that our first impressions influence later impressions. For instance when you take to a new acquaintance, you will probably discount, misinterpret or even ignore later contradictory information, unless they are too obvious to overlook.

Schemas can even help evoke expected behaviour in other people. For instance, if you believe that your new acquaintance is aggressive, you treat him as if he were really aggressive. In this way, your belief provokes his aggressiveness, which in turn reinforces your expectations. This circular process is known as the **self-fulfilling prophecy**.

Self-fulfilling prophecies can also be caused by stereotypes. Actually, a **stereotype** is a type of schema, one that is hard to get rid of, oversimplified, and not necessarily based on past experience. Attractiveness is a good example of what makes stereotypes self-fulfilling. Good looking people are usually perceived to be more socially skilled, more intelligent and funnier than those who are not so good looking. In result, they receive preferential treatment and are socially rewarded just for being attractive.

Decide if the following statements are true (T) or false (F).

1. First impressions are not stable and they change as soon as new information is acquired.
2. Schemas are hardly helpful because they make us categorise people easily and without much effort.
3. When you treat someone in a certain way, they may behave in ways that are in keeping with your expectations.
4. Self-fulfilling prophecy is the reason that good looking people are generally believed to possess many positive traits.

Exercise 2

Read the text and choose the correct option (*a*, *b* or *c*) for each gap.

Stereotypes

A stereotype is a generalised statement that we make about individuals because they belong to a particular group or type of people without regard to their own uniqueness. The ability to make generalised statements about others is our __________ (1) cognitive capacity, which allows us to make sense of the world around us and respond __________ (2) to it. If we were stripped of our ability to make generalised statements, we wouldn't be able to fall back on our intuition to __________ (3) the behaviour of other people, simply because we could never learn from the past and every social interaction would be a new experience. So, stereotypes are generally helpful, however they often have negative and unfair __________ (4). For example, most people believe that all politicians are corrupt and liars, although there are politicians who honestly work for their country. When people don't fit our __________ (5) ideas, we assume they are just an exception to the rule instead of challenging our stereotypes.

Unfavourable stereotyping usually leads to __________ (6) (a 'we and them' attitude), which in turn creates in-groups and out-groups, with out-groups being ____________ (7) negatively and __________ (8) against.

1. a) conditioned	b) hard-wired	c) determined
2. a) intuitively	b) attentively	c) effectively
3. a) provoke	b) affect	c) predict
4. a) implications	b) experiences	c) attributions
5. a) predisposed	b) prevalent	c) preconceived
6. a) schemas	b) prejudice	c) deviation
7. a) observed	b) noticed	c) viewed
8. a) discriminated	b) mistreated	c) victimised

Exercise 3

Complete the sentences below with the verbs from the box in the right form.

categorise, discount, cause, attach, form, break, make, conform

1. People __________ first impressions based mostly on appearance and the tone of voice and only slightly on what is actually said.

2. In some societies, social stigma __________ to homosexual behaviour often prevents gays from disclosing their orientation and makes them live behind closed doors.

3. Many tourists visiting Poland are surprised to see that Poles generally don't __________ to the national stereotype of heavy drinking ultracatholics.

4. On average, people tend to stick to their initial impressions and __________ later contradictions.

5. The teacher's attitude towards students may __________ self-fulfilling prophecies in education, since positive expectations can have favourable effects on students' academic performance.

6. People __________ one another by observing visible characteristics such as age, sex, race, nationality, socio-economic status, clothing, etc.

7. Once we __________ generalisations about people (e.g. 'she is weak', 'he is a snob'), we notice only the signs that confirm our judgement and reject those which don't.

8. Stereotypes are hard to __________ because our subjective and selective perception makes us see what we expect to see.

Exercise 4

Match the types of discrimination 1–6 with their descriptions a–f.

1. sexism
2. ageism
3. racism
4. ableism
5. classism
6. sizeism

a)
Judith has applied for more than 100 vacancies and been to more than 60 interviews, but has never scored a job offer. Now, at age 27 she is still unemployed but is not her CV that is failing her but her obesity or rather people's assumption that she is lazy and sloppy.

b)
A mob of teenagers were reported to have been involved in the assault on a man of Afghan origin in the centre of Berlin. The man was knocked down, punched and kicked repeatedly all over his body. If it weren't for a passerby who heard his call for help, the man would most certainly have been killed.

c)
Jake is not very popular at school and he is often teased by some of his classmates for not having a mobile phone and wearing hand-me-downs. Jack would love to fit in, but he comes from a poor family and his parents cannot afford anything better.

d)
A 39-year-old actress revealed in an interview that she was turned down for a role of love interest of a 56-year-old man. The role eventually went to her colleague eight years her junior.

It was not the first time that her age had been a barrier to being cast opposite male actors not only around her age but even a decade or so older.

e)
A disabled boy was unable to watch *The Theory of Everything*, a movie about the life of Stephen Hawking, at the Odeon Cinema in Harrogate, England. He was told that the movie was put in a screen without wheelchair accessible spaces and that there was no way to get his wheelchair into a screening.

f)
In the financial company where Sue works, the dress code requires women hired as secretaries and receptionists to wear smart clothes, high-heeled shoes (at least two inches high) and full make-up at all times. If any woman fails to meet the company's strict dress code demands she can be dismissed without notice. Surprisingly enough, the dress code for men isn't as strict.

14.

TEST YOURSELF

PART 1

Choose the best answer (*a, b, c* or *d*) which you think fits best.

1. A: 'I hear that Jim has been hit on his head. How is he doing?'

   B: 'He is still unconscious. He suffers what appears to be a severe __________.'

   a) contusion b) collision c) confusion d) concussion

2. A: 'Is that true that the new patient reports strong __________ hallucinations?'

   B: 'Yes, it is. He says that his food tastes metallic and that it's probably poisoned.'

   a) olfactory b) tactile c) gustatory d) haptic

3. A: 'How is your leg? Is it mending well?'

   B: 'It still hurts. Some days I think I need a __________ aid.'

   a) mobility b) motion c) moving d) malleable

4. A: 'I'm wondering why she has taken the job at that wage.'

   B: 'Probably because women are __________ to accept lower wages than men.'

   a) stimulated b) conditioned c) habituated d) reinforced

5. A: 'What is the name of the kid who played in *Home Alone*?'

B: 'Oh now, hold on. I knew it a minute ago, but it has __________ me.'

a) vanished b) erased c) escaped d) failed

6. A: 'Is the tumour __________, doctor?'

   B: 'I'm almost positive it isn't, but a biopsy must be performed, so that we can know for sure.'

   a) benign b) non-cancerous c) malignant d) gentle

7. A: 'Are you __________ motivated to work with at-risk youth or is it the incentives that you are after?'

   B: 'I don't care about incentives. I just love doing things I believe in.'

   a) intrinsically b) innocuously c) implicitly d) innately

8. A: 'How long has it been since you quit smoking?'

   B: 'Three years, but I still __________ a cigarette every now and then.'

   a) jones b) crave c) urge d) have

9. A: 'Is Mary getting better?'

   B: 'Her condition is in __________ now, and has been for almost three years.'

   a) relapse b) release c) retreat d) remission

10. A: 'When did you decide to __________ on fast foods?'

    B: 'Soon after watching *Supersize Me.* Have not missed them a bit.'

    a) go cold turkey c) chase the dragon
    b) have an old monkey d) fall prey

11. A: 'What do you usually do to __________ stress?'

    B: 'Going out into the fresh air helps. It clears my head.'

    a) relieve b) relive c) reprieve d) retrieve

12. A: 'Paul, what are your dreams like?'

    B: 'Well, they are __________ and confusing most of the time. I can't remember them for very long once I wake up.'

    a) vivid b) lucid c) latent d) vague

13. A: 'You did a great job on the IQ test. It __________ a score well above average, congratulations!'
B: 'Thanks, but I don't really believe in IQ tests. They aren't very reliable.'
a) yielded b) reflected c) scaled d) measured

14. A: 'Does coffee really make you more energetic? I can fall asleep with a cup of espresso in my hand!'
B: 'Yes, it helps me get through the day. Besides, it __________ my focus.'
a) releases b) evokes c) boosts d) inhibits

15. A: 'This song again? Really? Aren't you tired of it yet?'
B: 'No, I love it. It __________ so many memories.'
a) evokes b) retrieves c) exerts d) reminds

16. A: 'What did the biopsy show? What exactly is wrong with your liver?'
B: 'No one really knows. Liver conditions often go __________, you see.'
a) untreated b) mistreated c) undiagnosed d)misdiagnosed

17. A: 'What happened? Did she __________?'
B: 'They don't know yet, but she was found with a syringe in her arm.'
a) overdose b) overtake c) overdosage d) overdo

18. A: 'What was your reaction when you heard that you wouldn't see again?'
B: 'At first there was a lot of __________ but eventually I learnt to accept it.'
a) misbelief b) dysbelief c) unbelief d) disbelief

19. A: 'Is there any particular reason why you have a(n) __________ to fish?'
B: 'Yes, I got a fish bone stuck in my throat when I was young and it was there for two days!'
a) dislike b) aversion c) distaste d) allergy

20. A: 'Do you read reviews before watching a movie?'
B: 'I used to, but now I don't. I like to go to the pictures without any __________ ideas.'
a) preconceived b) discriminating c) prejudiced d) categorising

PART 2

Choose the best answer (*a, b, c* or *d*) which you think fits best.

1. Although memory __________ with age, memory loss is typically the result of a disease, not the ageing process.
   a) impairs b) discards c) declines d) vanishes
2. I've had __________ thoughts at times over the years, but I've never acted on them. It's not because I fear death, but because I have a responsibility to those I love and who love me back.
   a) suicide b) suicidal c) suicided d) suiciding
3. The abuse that John suffered at the hands of his father was so traumatic that he __________ the memory of it for many years.
   a) regressed b) released c) repressed d) retreated
4. After his sister was born, Peter __________ into being a baby again to get attention from his parents.
   a) reverted b) returned c) reversed d) recurred
5. We can remember the lyrics of songs we sang as children, yet sometimes we cannot successfully __________ more recent memories.
   a) store b) encode c) remind d) retrieve
6. Due to his __________ sleep pattern, Tony goes to sleep well past midnight and it's difficult to wake him up in the morning.
   a) affected b) disrupted c) influenced d) restrained
7. At first I was disturbed by the strange smell in the restaurant but after a few minutes I grew __________ to it and paid attention only to the food and my companions.
   a) accustomed b) used c) assimilated d) acquainted
8. Although many stroke patients are successfully rehabilitated, some of them are unable to regain complete functional independence and are left with a permanent disability, such as partial paralysis or __________ speech.
   a) stuttered b) mumbling c) babbling d) slurred

9. Even the mere thought of looking at someone eating messy food with their hands may __________ disgust in some people.
   a) reinforce b) exert c) elicit d) determine

10. Although they can appear charming and empathetic, psychopaths and sociopaths show a complete __________ for other people's feelings.
    a) neglect b) indifference c) disregard d) ignorance

11. The behaviourist perspective proposes that human nature is __________ and highly susceptible to environmental influences.
    a) fixed b) malleable c) constant d) shapely

12. The Binet-Simon Scale was developed to __________ less able from more able school children in order to provide the former with special education services.
    a) differentiate b) identify c) classify d) label

13. The __________ barrier helps block harmful chemicals from flowing into the foetus from the mother's blood.
    a) uterine b) umbilical c) amniotic d) placental

14. Partially sighted individuals need special __________________ devices (other than regular glasses) to use their remaining vision more effectively.
    a) optic b) optical c) vision d) visual

15. Defence mechanisms are devices employed by the ego to distort or __________ reality for the purpose of making it less threatening.
    a) falsify b) restrain c) prevent d) inhibit

16. Brain __________ revealed that the patient had suffered a massive stroke that destroyed about 70 percent of the left side of his brain.
    a) imagining b) imagery c) image d) imaging

17. Specialised sensory receptors __________ the energy of the stimulus into electrical signals and relay them to the brain.
    a) transfer b) transmit c) transduce d) transport

18. The noise level that initially seems too high soon becomes tolerable if you are repeatedly __________ to it.
a) paired b) stimulated c) conditioned d) exposed

19. When you enter a room with a clock ticking every second loudly, the sound may distract you, but before long you will __________ to respond to it.
a) cease b) adapt c) stop d) fail

20. Around the time of their first birthday, most babies __________ their first words.
a) develop b) utter c) communicate d) tell

21. Most people think of sleep as a 'time out', but in fact the __________ brain is very active as it is when we are awake.
a) asleep b) sleepy c) sleeping d) sleepless

22. If your behaviour is reinforced on a(n) __________ schedule, you may quickly lose interest in the reinforcer.
a) continuous b) intermittent c) variable d) fixed

23. According to Sigmund Freud, an infant who is __________ from breast-feeding too early may develop orally fixated habits such as overeating or thumb-sucking.
a) abstained b) ceased c) restrained d) weaned

24. In Albert Bandura's view, we learn __________ – that is by observing other people's actions and outcomes of these actions.
a) unconsciously b) vicariously c) reciprocally d) latently

25. In Pavlov's classic experiment, after several __________ of meat powder and bell, the dog came to salivate in response to hearing the bell.
a) presentations b) associations c) pairings d) stimuli

26. The ego seeks to __________ the id's desires and needs without violating the superego's demands.
a) gratify b) release c) alleviate d) mediate

PART 3

Choose the best answer (*a, b, c* or *d*) which you think fits best.

1. A woman has become obsessed with number 3. Whenever she washes her hands, she turns the tap on and off 3 times, gets 3 pumps of liquid soap and dries her hands 3 times. She also does other things in threes, including opening and closing doors. In all probability, the woman is suffering from __________ .

   a) schizophrenia
   b) bipolar disorder
   c) dissociative fugue
   d) OCD

2. Andrew has a drink problem. His family and friends realise that he is addicted, but when they confront him, he says: 'I may like to drink from time to time, but I'm not an alcoholic.' His behaviour best illustrates the defence mechanism called __________ .

   a) undoing
   b) sublimation
   c) reaction formation
   d) denial

3. Thomas hates it when his mom pesters him to make his bed. He eventually starts to make his bed as soon as he gets up to avoid his mom's nagging. The cessation of nagging represents __________ .

   a) positive reinforcement
   b) negative reinforcement
   c) positive punishment
   d) negative punishment

4. A mother tells her son to switch off the TV and go to sleep. After some time she is fairly certain that she can hear a faint buzzing sound of the television. Hearing the faint sound of the television is an example of __________ .

   a) absolute threshold
   b) difference threshold
   c) subliminal perception
   d) Weber's law

5. When asked what the sun is, 5-year-old Libby answered that it is a big ball that 'Daddy threw up into the air.' In Piagetian terms, Libby's response is an example of __________ .

a) animism
b) artificialism
c) egocentrism
d) conservation

6. You move into a new house close to a motorway. At first, you can't get a wink of sleep because of the traffic noise. After a few nights, however, you adjust. The noise is there, but it doesn't bother you as much. This process is called __________ .

a) classical conditioning
b) operant conditioning
c) sensory adaptation
d) habituation

7. My brother had those 'episodes' when he was a child. Each time he experienced them, he screamed in his sleep like he were on fire, pouring with sweat and thrashing out – an image I still can't shake off. When he woke up the next day he remembered nothing of it. Fortunately, he grew out of them by the time he was about 14. In all probability, the brother suffered from __________ .

a) hypnic jerks
b) somnambulism
c) night terrors
d) nightmares

8. Harriet is watching her favourite talent show on TV. After each performance, the camera takes the viewers backstage, where all the contestants are laughing and drinking a new brand of soft drink. The next day she goes to a shop where she sees the drink that was advertised on the show. She feels almost instantly good and buys it. In classical conditioning, the drink is a(n) __________.

a) neutral stimulus
b) unconditioned stimulus
c) conditioned stimulus
d) reflexive stimulus

9. A few nights ago you had a dream that you were flying high in the sky. You were told that a dream of flying indicates high hopes and a feeling that you are able to do things beyond your limitations. This analysis represents __________ of your dream.

a) latent content
b) wish fulfilment
c) universal dream
d) threat simulation

10. It's quite normal, though very annoying for a teacher, when a student falls

asleep in class. However, it's by no means normal when a teacher does so. A teacher's falling asleep in class may be due to __________ .

a) apnoea
b) narcolepsy
c) 'sleeping beauty' syndrome
d) circadian rhythm sleep disorder

11. Chris was unexpectedly laid off from the job he'd held down for many years. For weeks he looked for another job, but found none. Distraught, he started to drink. Initially it was only one or two drinks, but over time he noticed that it took more than three drinks to feel the alcohol's effect. Chris's body started to develop __________ .

a) withdrawal effects
b) cravings
c) tolerance
d) sensory accommodation

12. In a movie about him, Cristiano Ronaldo said: 'If we had two or three Cristiano Ronaldos in the team I would feel more comfortable.' Utterances of this kind and a strong belief that no one can outdo him suggest that the football player displays some traits of __________ .

a) sociopathy
b) narcissism
c) grandiose delusions
d) superego

13. A young man is brought to the emergency room by his parents because of a high fever, abdominal pain, diarrhoea and rhinorrhea. He appears malnourished and neglected. The patient's mother reports that he was taking drugs for 3 years until a few days ago when he quit abruptly. The patient symptoms suggest that he may be suffering from _________ .

a) drug tolerance
b) deliriums
c) anxiety disorder
d) withdrawal effects

14. A woman presented to the ER complaining of heart palpitations, stomach aches and dizziness. Countless medical tests were performed but none explained the woman's problems. In all probability, the woman's symptoms were _________ in nature.

a) psychosomatic
b) organic
c) somatic
d) physical

15. 7-month-old Susie enjoys the time when she is 'conversing' with her

mother. She says 'ba-ba-ba' and her mother responds with 'ba-ba-ba.' Susie's behaviour is referred to as _________ .

a) cooing
b) babbling
c) holophrasing
d) telegraphic speech

16. Following a viral infection of the brain, the man remembers very little. He is unable to form new long-term memories and has forgotten most of his past life, but he can still cook and perform other activities. The man can still cook because the virus didn't affect his _________ .

a) semantic memory
b) declarative memory
c) procedural memory
d) episodic memory

17. After a car accident which damaged his brain, Peter was no longer able to appropriately process his emotions. For instance, if held at gunpoint he wouldn't feel a pang of fear. The car accident damaged Peter's _________.

a) amygdala
b) medulla oblongata
c) hypothalamus
d) cerebellum

18. You retain a very brief smell of pizza after having walked by an Italian pizzeria, but it's gone immediately afterwards. The smell of pizza has been stored in your _________ .

a) sensory memory
b) short-time memory
c) flashbulb memory
d) semantic memory

19. When you first step in the lake, the water feels freezing cold to you. A few minutes later, however, you adapt and the water feels pleasantly cool. This adaptation to the water's temperature is what is called _________ .

a) habituation
b) sensory adaptation
c) sensation
d) classical conditioning

20. A football player fell to the ground after he was accidently hit in the head by an opponent's elbow. He was dazed for several seconds but soon he got up and was ready to return to the match. The coach however took him off the pitch and sent him to hospital for an examination. He did so because he suspected that the football player suffered a(n) _________.

a) aneurysm
b) tumour
c) concussion
d) haemorrhage

21. When you have entered a darkened movie theatre after being outdoors on a bright, sunny day you have difficulty seeing at first. You stumble down the aisle looking for your seat, but after a while you are able to see your way around. Your vision has improved as a result of ________ .

a) flashbulb memory
b) dark adaptation
c) habituation
d) accommodation

22. When Jenny was two years old, she learnt the word 'dog.' One day, as she was going in a car with her parents, she saw a fox running alongside the road and shouted happily 'doggy!' When her mother told her that it wasn't a dog but a fox, she became confused. The information didn't fit in with Jenny's belief that all four-legged animals are dogs and as a result she experienced ________ .

a) assimilation
b) incorporation
c) accommodation
d) disequilibrium

23. Your favourite jeans used to be dark blue. Now after a few years of wearing and washing they look faded out. Even though they have a great cut, you're not comfortable to wear them any more. The intensity of the colour of your jeans – dark blue or faded blue – refers to its ________ .

a) hue
b) brightness
c) saturation
d) purity

24. Your mother enjoys recounting your first experience of eating spaghetti at a restaurant. You were two at the time and got very messy with the dish. Your mother remembers it vividly, as though it was only yesterday, but you have no single recollection of it. This is an example of ________ .

a) infantile amnesia
b) memory decline
c) retrograde amnesia
d) memory lapse

25. Somebody calls you from an unfamiliar number. You try to ignore it, but because the phone keeps ringing, you eventually answer it. As soon as

you hear a voice speak up, you know that it's a friend of yours on the other end of the line. It turns out that he's calling from a borrowed phone because he has left his at home. Recognising your friend's voice is an example of _________ .

a) sensation
c) transduction
b) perception
d) adaptation

26. Last night I had a dream in which I was being chased by a huge man. Since I knew that I was asleep, I thought I might as well stop running and fight him. I grabbed the man from behind and put him in a choke hold, which made him pass out. Then I walked away, steering my dream into a more pleasant path. The dream I had last night is an example of a __________ dream.

a) latent
b) manifest
c) lucid
d) vague

27. When I shop, I must feel the fabric of the clothes I want to buy. If they don't feel nice on my skin, I put them back on hangers, no matter how good they look or who made them. The sense that is so important to me in my clothing shopping is called _________ .

a) gustation
b) olfaction
c) tactition
d) vision

28. Angie felt sick to her stomach after receiving a few chemotherapy treatments for breast cancer. She even felt nauseated when she smelled the treatment room or saw the IV needle. After the completion of treatment Angie got better, but the nausea reappeared for a while in response to the cues she associated with chemotherapy. The reappearance of nausea is an example of _________ .

a) extinction
c) unconditioning
b) spontaneous recovery
d) generalisation

29. Paul's room looks like a rubbish dump filled with food wrappers, plastic bags, old newspapers and other stuff which is buried underneath what you can see. The junk piles up and there is no end to it. It's even making it

outside the room into the hallway. Paul's room is evidence of _________.

a) hoarding
b) compulsive eating
c) compulsive shopping
d) drug abuse

30. A 61-year-old woman has lost her mobility and much of her mind. It all started with seemingly innocuous clumsiness and twitches, which progressively developed into the terrible disease that she is suffering from. The symptoms indicate that the woman is suffering from _________ .

a) Korsakoff's syndrome
b) Parkinson's disease
c) Alzheimer's disease
d) Huntington's disease

31. You've bought a bottle of Pepsi. The label says 'Drink Pepsi, Get Stuff' and tells you to remove the cap to see if you've won a prize. The message under the cap may be 'Congratulations! You've won a million dollars!' or 'Please, try again.' The schedule of reinforcement used by Pepsi is called _________ .

a) variable-interval schedule
b) variable-ratio schedule
c) fixed-interval schedule
d) fixed-ratio schedule

32. Joe would like to go out with his friends, but he knows that he should stay at home and revise for an exam the next day. Joe's struggle is between his _________ which makes him to want to have some fun and his _________, which tells him to stay in and study.

a) id, ego
b) ego, superego
c) id, superego
d) ego, id

33. Alice is very particular about cleanliness, especially in the kitchen. Even a few crumbs on the table can really drive her mad. According to the Freud's psychoanalytic theory, Alice is most likely fixated in the _______ stage.

a) phallic
b) anal
c) latency
d) oral

34. After watching a video on YouTube, Brian has learnt how to use an ice axe and walk with crampons. Now, he feels much more confident about

winter trekking. Brian has acquired new skills through ________ .

a) observational learning
b) vicarious reinforcement
c) operant conditioning
d) classical conditioning

35. Due to his fragile disposition, Michael tends to be sad or even depressed at times. According to Galen's theory of bodily fluids, Michael has a ________ temperament.

a) sanguine
b) choleric
c) phlegmatic
d) melancholic

36. Bridget was a nervous wreck as her maths exam approached. She spent more time and energy worrying about failing the exam than studying for it. As a result, she did poorly on the exam and failed indeed. Bridget's bad performance on the maths exam is an example of ________ .

a) primacy effect
b) negative stereotyping
c) self-fulfilling prophecy
d) preconceived ideas

KLUCZ

1. THE BRAIN

Ex. 1

1. F
2. F
3. F
4. T
5. T
6. T
7. F
8. F

Ex. 2

1. controls/regulates
2. Located
3. formed
4. relaying/transmitting
5. processes
6. consumes

Ex. 3

1. c
2. b

3. b
4. a
5. c
6. d
7. a

Ex. 4

1. head
2. traumatic
3. concussion
4. hemisphere
5. cortex
6. savant
7. neuroplasticity
8. workings

Ex. 5

BRAIN DISEASES					
Infections	Seizures	Trauma	Growth	Vascular Conditions	Neurodegenerative Conditions
meningitis, encephalitis, brain abscess	*epilepsy*	*concussion, (mild, moderate, severe) traumatic brain injury (TBI)*	*(malignant or benign) brain tumour*	*stroke, intracerebral haemorrhage, brain aneurysm, cerebral edema*	*Parkinson's disease, Huntington's disease, dementia, Alzheimer's disease*

Ex. 6

1. epilepsy
2. dementia/Alzheimer's disease

3. encephalitis
4. concussion
5. aneurysms
6. traumatic brain injury
7. tumour
8. intracerebral haemorrhage
9. stroke

2. SLEEP AND DREAMS

Ex. 1

1. vague
2. disturbing
3. meaningless
4. simulation
5. repressed
6. unconscious

Ex. 2

a)

1. e
2. g
3. b
4. h
5. a
6. d
7. c
8. f

b)

1. vague
2. waking
3. random

4. awake
5. universal
6. latent
7. repressed
8. bizarre

Ex. 3

1. sleeping
2. sleep
3. dream
4. sleep
5. sleep
6. dreaming
7. dreams, sleeping
8. Sleep

Ex. 4

1. recurring
2. random
3. vague
4. waking
5. repressed
6. Lucid

Ex. 5

1. lightly
2. twitches/spasms
3. Breathing/Respiration
4. rouse
5. strengthened/boosted

6. entering/reaching
7. night terrors/sleep terrors
8. sleepwalking/somnambulism
9. waking
10. vivid

N1→N2→N3→N2→REM→N2→N3 and so forth.

Ex. 6

1. c
2. b
3. f
4. g
5. a
6. d
7. e

3. SENSATION AND PERCEPTION

Ex. 1

1. F
2. F
3. T
4. T
5. F
6. T
7. T
8. T
9. T
10. F

Ex. 2

1. converted/transduced, relayed/transmitted
2. detected/registered
3. detect/register
4. processed
5. activated
6. respond

Ex. 3

a)
1. d
2. e
3. a
4. b
5. c

b)
1. tactile/haptic
2. gustatory
3. auditory
4. Optical
5. Visual/Vision
6. olfactory

Ex. 4

1. optical
2. visually, vision
3. vision
4. optical
5. visual
6. optic
7. Visual

Ex. 5

a)

1. constricts
2. dilates
3. focuses
4. contract
5. relax
6. projected

b)

1. strike
2. vibrate
3. amplifying
4. activate

c)

1. release
2. interact
3. dissolve
4. transports
5. produces

d)

1. regenerating
2. regulate
3. generate

Ex. 6

1. External stimuli enter the body through sensory organs.
2. Specialised cells (sensory receptors) don't respond to stimuli that are too weak to reach absolute threshold.
3. Sensory receptors convert stimulus energy into electrical signals.
4. Electrical signals are transmitted to the brain through specialised nerves.
5. The brain interprets electrical signals into meaningful information.
6. We gain knowledge of our environment through a process known as perception.

7. Our senses adapt to a stimulus that is presented continuously.
8. Most substances release odours into the air.
9. The epidermis is the protective barrier to harmful environmental factors.

Ex. 7

1. c
2. a
3. b
4. c
5. c
6. b
7. a
8. a

Ex. 8

1. absolute threshold
2. absolute threshold
3. difference threshold
4. Weber's law
5. difference threshold
6. subliminal perception
7. Weber's law
8. subliminal perception
9. difference threshold
10. difference threshold
11. subliminal perception
12. Weber's law

4. MEMORY

Ex. 1

1. a
2. c
3. d
4. b
5. d
6. b
7. a
8. c
9. a
10. c
11. a

Ex. 2

a)

Noun	Verb
retrieval	retrieve
retention	retain
storage	store
conversion	convert
recollection	recollect
recall	recall
rehearsal	rehearse
consolidation	consolidate
revision	revise
encoding	encode

b)

1. Retrieval
2. convert
3. consolidation
4. retains/restores
5. rehearsal/revision
6. stored
7. encoded
8. recall/recollect

Ex. 3

1. processes
2. commit
3. boosts
4. discards
5. decays
6. interfere
7. replays

Ex. 4

1. a
2. c
3. b
4. b
5. c
6. a
7. b

5. MEMORY LOSS

Ex. 1

1. F
2. T
3. F
4. T
5. F
6. F
7. T

Ex. 2

1. recall
2. form
3. erases
4. declines
5. devastate
6. Losing
7. has recovered
8. distorted
9. fails
10. escapes

Ex. 3

1. Memory loss
2. Memory lapses
3. Forgetfulness
4. Mild Cognitive Impairment
5. Dementia

Ex. 4

1. stabilise, cure
2. progresses
3. suffering
4. treat
5. appear
6. inhibit
7. affect

Ex. 5

1. a
2. c
3. b
4. a
5. b
6. a
7. c

Ex. 6

1. d
2. c
3. a
4. b
5. e

Ex. 7

1. dementia
2. forgetfulness
3. remember
4. lapses

5. ageing
6. disease
7. condition

6. LEARNING

Ex. 1

1. a
2. b
3. a
4. b
5. c
6. a
7. a
8. c

Ex. 2

1. operant conditioning, negative punishment
2. habituation
3. operant conditioning, negative reinforcement
4. operant conditioning, negative reinforcement
5. operant conditioning, positive reinforcement
6. habituation
7. classical conditioning
8. habituation
9. operant conditioning, positive punishment
10. classical conditioning

Ex. 3

a)

Verb	Noun
associate	association
elicit	elicitation
reinforce	reinforcement
acquire	acquisition
expose	exposure
interact	interaction
habituate	habituation
condition	conditioning
punish	punishment
modify	modification
reward	reward
terminate	termination

b)

1. conditioned
2. acquisition
3. terminates
4. elicit
5. habituate
6. reinforcement
7. exposed
8. rewarded
9. associate
10. interaction

Ex. 4

a)
1. unconditioned stimulus
2. unconditioned response
3. conditioned stimulus
4. neutral stimulus
5. unconditioned stimulus
6. conditioned response

b)
7. conditioned response
8. conditioned stimulus
9. unconditioned stimulus
10. conditioned response
11. conditioned stimulus

Ex. 5

a)
1. continuous
2. intermittent
3. ratio
4. interval
5. fixed
6. variable
7. fixed-ratio
8. variable-ratio
9. fixed-interval
10. variable-interval

b)
1. variable-interval schedule
2. variable-ratio schedule
3. fixed-ratio schedule
4. fixed-interval schedule

Ex. 6

1. mould
2. increase, decreases
3. evoke
4. learnt
5. accustom
6. exert
7. withheld
8. stimulated

Ex. 7

1. g
2. d
3. f
4. h
5. c
6. a
7. e
8. b

Ex. 8

1. exposed
2. elicit
3. aversion
4. learnt
5. reinforce/strengthen
6. conditioned

7. INTELLIGENCE

Ex. 1

1. c
2. b
3. a
4. a
5. a
6. c
7. a
8. b
9. c
10. b
11. b
12. c

Ex. 2

1. focused
2. measure
3. reflect
4. differentiate
5. neglecting
6. identify, label
7. yields
8. determining
9. stream
10. predict

Ex. 3

1. capacities
2. composite

3. entity, make-up
4. indicator
5. hallmarks
6. ratio
7. quotient

Ex. 4

1. developed
2. administered
3. adapted
4. revised
5. misused
6. discontinued

8. PERSONALITY

Ex. 1

1. a
2. b
3. a
4. d
5. c
6. b
7. c
8. a

Ex. 2

a. The superego, The superego
b. The id, The id
c. The superego, the id

d. The ego, the id
e. the ego, The ego
g. the id, The id
1. g
2. b
3. f
4. e
5. d
6. a
7. c

Ex. 3

1. temperament
2. fluids
3. types
4. trait
5. stereotypes

Ex. 4

1. traits
2. fixated, erogenous
3. latent
4. seeks
5. gratifying
6. slips
7. self-efficacy
8. drives

9. DEFENCE MECHANISMS

Ex. 1

1. devices/techniques
2. id's
3. superego's
4. unconsciousness/unconscious
5. Primitive/Immature
6. dealing
7. distort/falsify

Ex. 2

a. 7
b. 4
c. 8
d. 9
e. 1
f. 5
g. 6
h. 3
i. 10
j. 2

Ex. 3

1. reaction formation
2. rationalisation
3. displacement
4. isolation of affect
5. denial
6. regression

7. overcompensation
8. projection
9. sublimation
10. repression

Ex. 4

1. vent
2. lashing
3. blocked out
4. redirected
5. acknowledge
6. overcompensate
7. channelled
8. retreated
9. make
10. justify
11. project
12. regressing
13. distanced

Ex. 5

1. relieve
2. operate
3. negates
4. reduce
5. cope
6. substitutes
7. distort

10. MENTAL ILLNESS

Ex. 1

1. T
2. T
3. F
4. F
5. F
6. T

Ex. 2

a)

excessive worry, auditory hallucinations, emotional numbness, restrictive eating, ritualistic behaviours, partial paralysis, pounding heart, suicidal thoughts, intrusive thoughts, mood swings

b)

1. excessive worry – GAD
2. restrictive eating – eating disorder
3. ritualistic behaviours, intrusive thoughts – OCD
4. auditory hallucinations – schizophrenia
5. mood swings, suicidal thoughts – bipolar disorder
6. pounding heart – social phobia
7. partial paralysis – conversion disorder
8. emotional numbness – PTSD

c)

1. period of recovery – remission
2. craze – frenzy
3. acute – severe
4. somatic – physical
5. recurrent recollections – flashbacks

Ex. 3

1. paranoid delusions, slurred speech
2. gustatory hallucinations
3. Social withdrawal
4. racing thoughts
5. hot flashes
6. low mood
7. erratic behaviours
8. grandiose sense of self-importance
9. thought insertion
10. dry mouth
11. catatonic stupor
12. word salad

Ex. 4

1. at
2. to
3. for
4. by, from
5. to
6. with, through
7. with, with
8. to
9. to
10. in, to

Ex. 5

1. disrupting
2. exacerbates
3. affect
4. overlap

5. strikes
6. mimic
7. triggers
8. relapsed

Ex. 6

a)

Prefix	Example Words
ab	abnormal
anti	antidepressant, antipsychotic, antianxiety
dis	disregard, disinhibited, disability, distrustful
dys	dysfunction
il	illegal
im	imbalance, immobility
in	insane, instability, inability, incurable, incoherent
ir	irrational, irresponsible
mal	maladaptive, malformed, malfunction, malnourished
mis	misuse, misdiagnose
un	unpredictable, unstable, unable, uninhibited

b)

1. misuse/abuse
2. abnormal
3. instability
4. incoherent

5. irrational
6. unstable, misdiagnosed
7. maladaptive
8. dysfunction/malfunction
9. immobility
10. disregard
11. insane
12. malnourished

Ex. 7

1. h
2. e
3. f
4. b
5. a
6. d
7. c
8. g

11. ADDICTION

Ex. 1

1. a
2. a
3. c
4. b
5. b
6. c
7. a
8. b
9. c
10. b

Ex. 2

1. dependent
2. making
3. addicted
4. practice
5. often
6. bad
7. predisposition
8. restrain
9. loss
10. kick

Ex. 3

1. started drinking
2. I am no longer dependent
3. relapsed
4. became addicted to
5. quit
6. quit abruptly
7. Reducing
8. took an overdose
9. craving
10. intoxicated by
11. was inebriated
12. smoking

Ex. 4

1. b
2. c
3. d
4. a

Ex. 5

1. gamblers
2. alcohol abuser
3. workaholic
4. compulsive eater
5. heavy smoker
6. compulsive shopper
7. compulsive hoarders
8. drug addict
9. caffeine addict
10. webaholic

Ex. 6

1. nausea
2. diarrhoea
3. lacrimation
4. myalgia
5. pupillary dilation
6. abdominal cramping
7. hyperalgesia
8. rhinorrhea

12. HUMAN DEVELOPMENT

Ex. 1

1. F
2. T
3. F
4. T
5. T
6. F

7. T
8. F

Ex. 2

1. fertilised
2. implants
3. develops
4. discharges
5. floats
6. form
7. discern
8. shifting

Ex. 3

a)

Noun	Adjective
uterus	uterine
placenta	placental
amnion	amniotic
umbilicus	umbilical
foetus	foetal
embryo	embryonic
pupil	pupillary
reflex	reflexive

b)

1. amnion
2. foetal

3. reflexive
4. umbilicus
5. uterine
6. embryonic
7. placental
8. pupils

Ex. 4

1. b
2. c
3. a
4. b
5. c
6. a
7. a
8. b

Ex. 5

1. reverse
2. ceases
3. acquire
4. reason, experience
5. construct
6. organise
7. conserve

Ex. 6

1. c
2. b
3. a

4. e
5. d

Ex. 7

a)

1. imitating
2. utterances
3. mastery
4. hard-wired
5. utter
6. combining
7. absorbing

b)

1. T
2. T
3. T
4. F
5. F
6. F
7. F
8. T

c)

- language acquisition must occur by puberty, otherwise a child will never achieve a full command of language
- single words
- putting two words together in simple, laconic sentences
- a rapid expansion of children's vocabulary

Ex. 8

a)

1. g
2. d

3. a
4. h
5. i
6. b
7. e
8. c

b)

1. put two words together
2. expand their repertoire of words
3. accumulates 200 words
4. speaking in complete, ... , sentences
5. detect differences in word order
6. use gestures and vocalisations
7. develop language skills
8. communicate their thoughts

13. SOCIAL PSYCHOLOGY

Ex. 1

1. F
2. F
3. T
4. T

Ex. 2

1. b
2. a
3. c
4. a
5. c
6. b

7. c
8. a

Ex. 3

1. form
2. attached
3. conform
4. discount
5. cause
6. categorise
7. make
8. break

Ex. 4

a. 6
b. 3
c. 5
d. 2
e. 4
f. 1

14. TEST YOURSELF

Part 1

1. d
2. c
3. a
4. b
5. c
6. c

7. a
8. b
9. d
10. a
11. b
12. d
13. a
14. c
15. a
16. c
17. a
18. d
19. b
20. a

Part 2

1. c
2. b
3. c
4. a
5. d
6. b
7. a
8. d
9. c
10. c
11. b
12. a
13. d
14. b
15. a
16. d
17. c

18. d
19. a
20. b
21. c
22. a
23. d
24. b
25. c
26. a

Part 3

1. d
2. d
3. b
4. a
5. b
6. d
7. c
8. c
9. a
10. b
11. c
12. b
13. d
14. a
15. b
16. c
17. a
18. a
19. b
20. c
21. b
22. d

23. c
24. a
25. b
26. c
27. c
28. b
29. a
30. d
31. b
32. c
33. b
34. a
35. d
36. c

SŁOWNIK

Skróty

cf.	porównaj
n.	rzeczownik
plur.	liczba mnoga
syn.	synonim
v.	czasownik

A

abdominal cramping kurcze w jamie brzusznej

ableism handicapizm, dyskryminacja wobec osób niepełnosprawnych

abnormal nienormalny, nieprawidłowy

abrasion otarcie

abstain (from) powstrzymywać się (od)

abstinence abstynencja

abuse (*n.*) nadużywanie (np. alkoholu); wykorzystywanie, znęcanie się, molestowanie; **alcohol abuse** nadużywanie alkoholu; **drug abuse** nadużywanie środków farmakologicznych

abuse (*v.*) nadużywać, wykorzystywać, znęcać się, molestować

abuser osoba uzależniona; **alcohol abuser** osoba nadużywająca alkoholu; **drug abuser** osoba nadużywająca narkotyków, narkoman

accommodation akomodacja

accumulate gromadzić, kumulować

accustomed (to) przyzwyczajony (do)

acknowledge przyznać (się), potwierdzać

acquainted zaznajomiony, oswojony

acquire przyswajać, zdobywać

acquisition przyswajanie, zdobywanie

acute (*syn.* **severe**) ostry

adapt (to) przystosowywać (się), dostosowywać się (do czegoś)

adaptation adaptacja, przystosowanie (się); **dark adaptation** adaptacja do ciemności; **light adaptation** adaptacja do światła; **sensory adaptation** adaptacja sensoryczna

addict nałogowiec, osoba uzależniona

addicted (to) (*syn.* **dependent, hooked**) uzależniony (od)

addiction uzależnienie; **behavioural addiction** uzależnienie behawioralne (czynnościowe); **substance addiction** uzależnienie od substancji psychoaktywnych

addictive uzależniający

adolescence adolescencja, okres dorastania

adulthood dorosłość, okres dorosłości

aetiology etiologia, przyczyna

affect (*n.*) afekt; **isolation of affect** izolacja afektu

affect (*v.*) oddziaływać, mieć wpływ

age wiek; **chronological age** wiek życia; **mental age** wiek umysłowy

ageism ageizm, dyskryminacja ze względu na wiek

airways drogi oddechowe

alcohol poisoning zatrucie alkoholowe

alertness czujność

alter (*syn.* **modify**) zmieniać, modyfikować

amnesia amnezja; **anterograde amnesia** amnezja/niepamięć następczna, anterograda; **infantile amnesia** (*or* **childhood amnesia**) amnezja dziecięca; **retrograde amnesia** amnezja/niepamięć wsteczna, retrograda

amnion owodnia

amniotic fluid płyn owodniowy

amniotic sac worek owodniowy

amplify wzmacniać

amplitude amplituda

amygdala jądro migdałowate, ciało migdałowate

animism animizm

animistic thinking myślenie animistyczne

anorexia nervosa jadłowstręt psychiczny, anoreksja

anterior przedni

antidepressants antydepresanty

antipsychotics (*syn.* **neuroleptics**) leki przeciwpsychotyczne, neuroleptyki

anvil (*or* **incus**) kowadełko

anxiety niepokój, lęk

anxiolytic lek przeciwlękowy, anksjolityk

apnoea bezdech

artificialism artyficjalizm

assimilation asymilacja

associate kojarzyć

audition (*or* **sense of hearing**) zmysł słuchu, słuch

auditory słuchowy

aversion (to) wstręt, awersja (do)

awareness świadomość

B

babble gaworzyć

basal ganglia jądra podstawne, jądra podstawy

bedwetting (*or* **nocturnal enuresis**) moczenie nocne

behaviour zachowanie; **abnormal behaviour** nieprawidłowe zachowanie;

erratic behaviour chaotyczne zachowanie; **ritualistic behaviour** zachowanie rytualne

benign łagodny

bias uprzedzenie, tendencyjność

bile żółć, **black bile** czarna żółć; **yellow bile** żółta żółć

blank slate niezapisana tablica

blindness ślepota

block out zapominać

blood pressure ciśnienie krwi

blood vessel naczynie krwionośne

blurry (*syn.* **vague**) mglisty, niewyraźny

boost wzmacniać, poprawiać

bounce (off sth) odbijać się (od)

brain mózg; **brainstem** (lub **brain stem**) pień mózgu; **midbrain** śródmózgowie; **reward circuitry of the brain** układ nagrody w mózgu, mózgowy układ nagrody

brain abscess ropień mózgu

brain activity aktywność mózgu

brain aneurysm tętniak mózgu

brain function funkcja mózgu

brain imaging obrazowanie mózgu

brain tumour guz mózgu

breastfeeding karmienie piersią

breathing oddychanie

brightness jasność koloru

bulimia nervosa (BN) żarłoczność psychiczna, bulimia

C

capacity zdolność; pojemność

catalyst katalizator

catatonic stupor katatoniczny stupor (osłupienie)

cavity jama; **nasal cavity** jama nosowa; **oral cavity** jama ustna

cease przestawać, kończyć

cell komórka; **ganglion cell** komórka zwojowa; **glial cell** (*or* **glia**) komórka glejowa; **hair cell** komórka rzęsata; **nerve cell** (*or* **neuron**) komórka nerwowa

cell division podział komórki

cerebellum móżdżek

cerebral edema obrzęk mózgu

cerebrum kresomózgowie

childhood dzieciństwo, okres dzieciństwa

choleric choleryczny

ciliary muscle mięsień rzęskowy

cilium (*plur.* **cilia**) rzęska

circulatory system układ krążenia

classism dyskryminacja klasowa

cocaine kokaina; **crack cocaine** krak

cochlea ślimak

cognition poznanie; **social cognition** poznanie społeczne

cognitive poznawczy, kognitywny

combine łączyć

communicate przekazywać, komunikować

complex kompleks; **Electra complex** kompleks Elektry; **Oedipus complex** kompleks Edypa

composite kompozyt, zbiór

compulsion przymus, natręctwo

compulsive natrętny, kompulsywny

compulsive eater osoba uzależniona od jedzenia

compulsive hoarder nałogowy zbieracz

compulsive shopper osoba uzależniona od zakupów

compulsive shopping kupowanie kompulsywne, zakupoholizm

compulsive texting kompulsywne wysyłanie SMS-ów

computed tomography scan (CT) tomografia komputerowa

concussion wstrząśnienie mózgu

condition (*syn.* **disease**, **disorder**, **illness**) choroba, zaburzenie; stan; **neurodegenerative condition** choroba neurodegeneracyjna; **vascular condition** choroba naczyniowa

conditioning warunkowanie; **classical conditioning** warunkowanie klasyczne; **operant conditioning** warunkowanie instrumentalne

cone czopek

conscious świadomy, przytomny

consciousness świadomość, przytomność

conservation stałość

consistent stały, konsekwentny

consolidate utrwalać, konsolidować

consonant spółgłoska

constrict zwężać (się)

content treść; **latent content** ukryta treść; **manifest content** jawna treść

contract (a disease) nabawiać się (choroby), zachorować; kurczyć (się)

contraction skurcz, zwarcie

contradiction sprzeczność

convert przekształcać

coo gruchać

cornea rogówka

corpus callosum ciało modzelowate

cortex kora; **cerebral cortex** kora mózgowa; **olfactory cortex** kora węchowa; **prefrontal cortex** kora przedczołowa; **somatosensory cortex** kora czuciowo-somatyczna

CPAP (**continuous positive airway pressure**) **machine** aparat do bezdechu sennego CPAP

craving pragnienie

crawl pełzać

critical period okres krytyczny

D

debilitating osłabiający, wyniszczający

decay zanikać, słabnąć

defence mechanism mechanizm obronny

delirium majaczenie

delivery rozwiązanie ciąży

delta wave fala delta

delusion urojenie; **paranoid delusions** urojenia paranoiczne

dementia otępienie, demencja; **Lewy body dementia** otępienie z ciałami Lewy'ego; **vascular dementia** otępienie naczyniowe

denial zaprzeczenie

deny zaprzeczać

dependency uzależnienie

dependent (on) (*syn*. **addicted, hooked**) zależny, uzależniony (od)

depressants depresanty

depressed przygnębiony, osowiały, w depresji

depression depresja, przygnębienie

depth głębia

dermis skóra właściwa

detect wyczuwać, wykrywać

deteriorate pogarszać się, podupadać

determine określać, ustalać

development rozwój; **cognitive development** rozwój poznawczy; **locomotor development** rozwój ruchowy

deviance dewiacja

device urządzenie, przyrząd; **optical device** przyrząd optyczny, urządzenie optyczne

diagnose (*n.*) diagnoza, rozpoznanie

diagnose (*v.*) diagnozować, rozpoznawać

diarrhoea biegunka

differentiate różnicować, odgraniczać

dilate rozszerzać (się)

disability niepełnosprawność

discard usuwać, pozbywać się

discharge wydzielać

discrimination dyskryminacja

disease (*syn.* **condition**, **disorder**, **illness**) choroba; **Alzheimer's disease (AD)** choroba Alzheimera; **Creutzfield-Jakob disease (CJD)** choroba Creutzfielda-Jakoba; **Huntington's disease (HD)** pląsawica Huntingtona, choroba Huntingtona; **Parkinson's disease (PD)** choroba Parkinsona

disequilibrium nierównowaga

disinhibited nieskrępowany

disorder (*syn.* **condition**, **disease**, **illness**) zaburzenie, choroba; **antisocial personality disorder (APD)** antyspołeczne zaburzenie osobowości; **anxiety disorder** zaburzenie lękowe; **bipolar disorder** zaburzenie dwubiegunowe; **borderline personality disorder (BPD)** graniczne zaburzenie osobowości; **circadian rhythm sleep disorder (CRSD)** zaburzenie rytmu dobowego; **cognitive disorder** zaburzenie poznawcze; **conversion disorder (CD)** zaburzenie konwersyjne; **dissociative disorder** zaburzenie dysocjacyjne, **eating disorder** zaburzenie odżywiania; **generalised anxiety disorder (GAD)** uogólnione zaburzenie lękowe; **major depressive disorder (MDD)** znaczna depresja; **mental disorder** choroba psychiczna; **mood disorder** zaburzenie afektywne (nastroju); **narcissistic personality disorder (NPD)** narcystyczne zaburzenie osobowości; **obsessive-compulsive disorder (OCD)** zaburzenie obsesyjno-kompulsywne; **panic disorder (PD)** lęk paniczny; **personality disorder (PD)** zaburzenie osobowości; **post-traumatic stress disorder (PTSD)** zespół stresu pourazowego; **sleep disorder** zaburzenie snu; **substance use disorder** zaburzenie związane z zażywaniem substancji

displacement przemieszczenie

disregard nie zwracać uwagi, ignorować

disrupt zaburzać, zakłócać

disruption zakłócenie, przerwanie

dissociative dysocjacyjny

dissociative fugue fuga dysocjacyjna

dissolve rozpuszczać

distance (from) dystansować się (od)

distort wypaczać, zniekształcać

distrustful nieufny, podejrzliwy

disturbed niezrównoważony, upośledzony; **mentally disturbed** upośledzony umysłowo

dizziness zawroty głowy

doped (up) (on) pod wpływem narkotyku lub alkoholu

dream (*n.*) marzenie senne, sen; **lucid dream** sen świadomy; **vivid dream** intensywne marzenie senne

dream (*v.*) śnić

drowsy (*syn.* **somnolent**) senny

drug addict narkoman

dry mouth suchość błony śluzowej jamy ustnej

dysfunction dysfunkcja

dysregulation rozregulowanie

E

ear ucho; **inner ear** ucho wewnętrzne; **middle ear** ucho środkowe; **outer ear** ucho zewnętrzne

eardrum (*or* **tympanic membrane**) bębenek

ease łagodzić, koić, uśmierzać

echolocation echolokacja

ego (*cf.* **id**, **superego**) ego (ja, jaźń), w psychoanalizie jeden z trzech komponentów osobowości

egocentrism egocentryzm

elicit wywoływać, uzyskać

elicitation uzyskanie

embryo embrion, zarodek

embryonic embrionalny, zarodkowy

empathy empatia

encephalitis zapalenie mózgu

encode kodować

encoding kodowanie

entity byt

environmental środowiskowy

epidermis naskórek, epiderma

epilepsy padaczka, epilepsja

equilibrium równowaga

erase wymazać, usunąć

erogenous zone strefa erogenna

evoke wywoływać, przywoływać

exacerbate pogarszać, potęgować

examination badanie, oględziny

excessive worry nadmierny niepokój

exert wywierać

exhibitionism ekshibicjonizm

experience doświadczenie, przeżycie

explore badać, rozpoznawać

expose (to) narazić, wystawiać (na coś)

exposure (to) wystawienie (się) (na), narażenie

extinction wygasanie

eye oko

F

facial expressions mimika

falsify fałszować

fatigue zmęczenie, znużenie

fertilised zapłodniony

foetal płodowy

foetus płód

fever gorączka, temperatura

fixation fiksacja

fixed stały, ustalony

flashback retrospekcja

flavour smak

focus ogniskować

forget zapominać

forgetfulness zapominalstwo

form tworzyć

fovea dołek siatkówki oka

frenzy szał

frigidity oziębłość

function word funktor

functional magnetic resonance imaging (**fMRI**) funkcjonalne obrazowanie metodą rezonansu magnetycznego, funkcjonalny rezonans magnetyczny

G

gambler hazardzista

generate wzbudzać, wywoływać

genetic make-up kod genetyczny

gestation ciąża

glia (*or* **glial cell**) glej

grandiosity megalomania

gratification zaspokojenie, zadowolenie, gratyfikacja

gratify zaspokajać, zadowalać

grey matter substancja szara, istota szara

growth narośl

gustation (*or* **sense of taste**) zmysł smaku, smak

gustatory smakowy

H

habit nawyk, przyzwyczajenie, nałóg

habituate przyzwyczajać (się)

habituation habituacja, przyzwyczajenie

hair follicle mieszek włosowy

hallmark cecha charakterystyczna

hallucination omam, halucynacja; **auditory hallucinations** halucynacje słuchowe; **gustatory hallucinations** halucynacje smakowe; **olfactory hallucinations** halucynacje węchowe

hammer (*or* **malleus**) młoteczek

haptic (*syn.* **tactile**) dotykowy

hard-wired (*syn.* **inborn**, **innate**) wrodzony

head trauma uraz głowy

heart palpitations kołatanie serca

heart rate rytm zatokowy

heavy smoker nałogowy palacz

hemisphere półkula mózgu

hereditary dziedziczny

heroin heroina

herpes simple virus wirus opryszczki pospolitej

hippocampus (*pl.* **hippocampi**) hipokamp

holophrasis (*pl.* **holophrases**) holofraza (wypowiedź jednowyrazowa)

hooked (on) (*syn.* **addicted**, **dependent**) uzależniony (od)

hormonal fluctuations wahania hormonalne

hot flashes uderzenia gorąca

hue odcień

humour humor, jeden z podstawowych płynów ciała

hyperactivity nadczynność

hyperalgesia nadwrażliwość na ból, przeczulica, hiperalgezja

hyperthymesia hipermnezja, wybitna pamięć autobiograficzna

hypnic jerk mimowolny skurcz mięśni (któremu zwykle towarzyszy uczucie spadania)

hypnotic lek nasenny

hypodermis (*or* **subcutaneous tissue**) tkanka podskórna

hypothalamus podwzgórze

I/J/K

iatrogenic jatrogenny

id (*cf*. **ego**, **superego**) id (ono), w psychoanalizie jeden z trzech komponentów osobowości

illness (*syn*. **condition**, **disease**, **disorder**) choroba

imbalance brak równowagi, nierówność

imitate (*syn*. **mimic**) naśladować

immobility niemożność poruszania się, znieruchomienie

immoral niemoralny

immune system system odpornościowy, system immunologiczny

impair upośledzać, pogarszać

impaired upośledzony; **visually impaired** niedowidzący, słabowidzący

impairment upośledzenie, uszkodzenie, zaburzenie; **mild cognitive impairment (MCI)** łagodne zaburzenia poznawcze; **speech impairment** zaburzenie mowy; **visual/vision impairment** zaburzenie widzenia, wada wzroku

impression wrażenie, doznanie

inability niezdolność, nieumiejętność

inadequate nieadekwatny

inborn (*syn*. **hard-wired**, **innate**) wrodzony

incoherent niespójny, bełkotliwy

incorporate wcielać, włączać

incurable nieuleczalny

incus (*or* **anvil**) kowadełko

indicator wyznacznik, wykładnik

induce wywoływać, powodować

inebriated (*syn.* **intoxicated**) nietrzeźwy

infancy niemowlęctwo, okres niemowlęcy

infant niemowlę

infection zakażenie, infekcja

ingestion przyjmowanie, przyswajanie

inhalation wdychanie

inhibit hamować, spowalniać

injection wstrzykiwanie

injury uraz; **traumatic brain injury (TBI)** urazowe uszkodzenie mózgu

innate (*syn.* **hard-wired**, **inborn**) wrodzony

innocuous nieszkodliwy

insane niepoczytalny, obłąkany

insight (into) wgląd (w); wnikliwość, intuicja

insomnia bezsenność

instability chwiejność, niestabilność

intelligence inteligencja; **crystallised intelligence** inteligencja skrystalizowana; **emotional intelligence** inteligencja emocjonalna; **fluid intelligence** inteligencja płynna; **'g' intelligence** inteligencja ogólna; **multiple intelligences** inteligencja wieloraka

interfere zaburzać, zakłócać

internal wewnętrzny

intoxicated (*syn.* **inebriated**) nietrzeźwy

intoxication nietrzeźwość

intracerebral haemorrhage krwotok śródmózgowy

intrinsic wewnętrzny, wewnątrzpochodny

invertebrate bezkręgowce

involuntary mimowolny, bezwiedny

IQ test test inteligencji

iris tęczówka

irrational irracjonalny

just noticeable difference (jnd) ledwo dostrzegalna różnica

justify uzasadniać, usprawiedliwiać

knowledge wiedza

L

label (*n.*) etykieta

label (*v.*) oznaczać, określać mianem

laconic lakoniczny, lapidarny

lacrimation łzawienie

language język

language acquisition device (LAD) mechanizm przyswajania języka

lash out (at sb) naskakiwać (na kogoś)

latent ukryty, utajony

law prawo; **Weber's law** prawo Webera

learning uczenie (się)

lens soczewka

lethargy letarg, marazm

limb kończyna

limbic system układ limbiczny

limen (*or* **threshold**) próg

lobe płat; **frontal lobe** płat czołowy; **occipital lobe** płat potyliczny; **parietal lobe** płat ciemieniowy; **temporal lobe** płat skroniowy

locomotor lokomocyjny, ruchowy

loudness głośność

low mood przygnębienie

M

magnetic resonance imaging (MRI) obrazowanie metodą rezonansu magnetycznego, rezonans magnetyczny

maladaptive źle przystosowany

malformed zdeformowany

malfunction niewydolność

malignant złośliwy

malleable plastyczny

malleus (*or* **hammer**) młoteczek

malnourished niedożywiony

maltreat maltretować, znęcać się

mania mania

manic maniakalny

marijuana marihuana

mastery władanie (językiem), biegłość

mature dojrzewać

medulla oblongata rdzeń przedłużony, rdzeniomózgowie

melancholic melancholik

membrane błona; **basilar membrane** błona podstawowa; **tympanic membrane** (*or* **eardrum**) błona bębenkowa

memory pamięć; **autobiographical memory** pamięć autobiograficzna; **echoic memory** pamięć echoiczna; **episodic memory** pamięć epizodyczna; **iconic memory** pamięć ikoniczna; **explicit memory** (**declarative**) pamięć jawna (pamięć deklaratywna); **flashbulb memory** pamięć fleszowa; **implicit memory** (**procedural**) pamięć utajona, ukryta (pamięć proceduralna); **long-term memory** pamięć długotrwała; **semantic memory** pamięć semantyczna; **sensory memory** pamięć sensoryczna; **short-term memory** pamięć krótkotrwała; **spatial memory** pamięć przestrzenna

memory lapse zanik pamięci, luka w pamięci

memory loss utrata pamięci

meningitis zapalenie opon mózgowo-rdzeniowych

mental mentalny, psychiczny

microvillus (*plur*. **microvilli**) mikrokosmek

mimic (*syn*. **imitate**) naśladować

mind umysł

misdiagnose błędnie diagnozować, źle rozpoznać

misdiagnosed (*cf*. **undiagnosed**) błędnie zdiagnozowany

mistreat źle traktować

misuse nadużywać

mitosis mitoza, podział komórkowy

mobility aid urządzenie wspomagające przemieszczanie się

modify (*syn*. **alter**) zmieniać, modyfikować

molecule cząsteczka, molekuła

mood stabiliser stabilizator nastroju

mood swings huśtawka nastrojów, zmienność nastrojów

morphine morfina

mould formować, kształtować

multiple sclerosis stwardnienie rozsiane

muscle control kontrola mięśni

myalgia mięśnioból, ból mięśniowy

N

narcissism narcyzm

narcissist narcyz

narcolepsy narkolepsja

nausea mdłości, nudności

nearsightedness krótkowzroczność

negate negować, przeczyć

nerve nerw; **auditory nerve** nerw słuchowy; **cranial nerve** nerw czaszkowy; **facial nerve** nerw twarzowy; **glossopharyngeal nerve** nerw językowo-gardłowy; **olfactory nerve** nerw węchowy; **optic nerve** nerw wzrokowy; **vagus nerve** nerw błędny

nerve fiber włókno nerwowe

neural network sieć neuronowa

neuroleptics (*syn.* **antipsychotics)** leki przeciwpsychotyczne, neuroleptyki

neuron (*or* **nerve cell**) neuron

neuroplasticity neuroplastyczność (plastyczność mózgu)

newborn noworodek

nicotine nikotyna

nicotine patch plaster antynikotynowy

night terrors (*or* **sleep terrors**) lęki nocne

nocturnal enuresis (*or* **bedwetting**) moczenie nocne

nose nos

nostril nozdrze

numbness odrętwienie

nutrients substancje odżywcze

O

object permanence stałość przedmiotu

observational learning uczenie się obserwacyjne

OD (*or* **overdose**) przedawkować

olfaction (*or* **sense of smell**) zmysł węchu, węch

olfactory węchowy

olfactory bulb opuszka węchowa

olfactory epithelium nabłonek węchowy

opiate opiat

optic wzrokowy, oczny, optyczny

optical wzrokowy, optyczny

organic organiczny

ossicles kosteczki słuchowe

oval window okienko przedsionka

overcompensate (for) kompensować

overcompensation kompensacja

overdose (*v*. *or* **OD**) przedawkować

overdose (*n*.) nadmierna dawka

overlap nakładać się

oxygen tlen

P/Q

papilla (*plur*. **papillae**) brodawka

partial paralysis częściowy paraliż

perceive postrzegać

perception postrzeganie, percepcja; **subliminal perception** percepcja podprogowa

phlegm limfa

phlegmatic flegmatyczny

phobia fobia; **social phobia** fobia społeczna

photoreceptor fotoreceptor

physiological fizjologiczny

pinna małżowina uszna

pins and needles mrowienie

pitch wysokość dźwięku

placenta łożysko

placental łożyskowy

plight trudne położenie

pons most

positron emission tomography (PET) pozytonowa tomografia emisyjna

post-mortem autopsja

posture postawa, postura

pounding heart kołatanie serca

predispose (to) predysponować (do)

prejudice uprzedzenie

prenatal prenatalny

preschooler dziecko w okresie przedszkolnym

primacy effect efekt pierwszeństwa

principle zasada; **pleasure principle** zasada przyjemności; **reality principle** zasada rzeczywistości

process przetwarzać

project (sth onto sb) projektować (coś na kogoś)

projection projekcja

psychopathology psychopatologia

psychosomatic psychosomatyczny

psychotherapy psychoterapia

psychotic psychotyczny

puberty okres dojrzewania, pokwitanie

punishment kara; **negative punishment** kara negatywna; **positive punishment** kara pozytywna

pupil źrenica

pupillary dilation rozszerzenie źrenic

quit rzucać

quotient iloraz; **intelligence quotient (IQ)** iloraz inteligencji

R

racism rasizm

random losowy, przypadkowy

ratio wskaźnik, współczynnik

rationalisation racjonalizacja

reaction formation reakcja upozorowana

reason rozumować

recall (*n.*) pamięć, przypominanie

recall (*v. syn.* **recollect, remember**) pamiętać, przypominać sobie

receptor receptor; **sensory receptor** receptor czuciowy, sensoryczny

reciprocal determinism determinizm wzajemny

recollect (*syn.* **recall**, **remember**) przypominać sobie

recover wyzdrowieć

recurring powracający

redirect przekierowywać

reflex odruch; **Moro reflex** odruch Moro; **parachute reflex** odruch spadochronowy; **postural reflexes** odruchy posturalne; **righting reflexes** odruchy prostowania; **rooting reflex** odruch szukania; **sucking reflex** odruch ssania

reflexive odruchowy

regenerate odnawiać, regenerować

regress cofać się

regression regresja

regulate kontrolować, regulować

rehearse powtarzać

reinforce wzmacniać

reinforcement wzmocnienie; **continuous reinforcement** wzmacnianie ciągłe; **intermittent reinforcement** wzmacnianie przerywane; **negative reinforcement** wzmocnienie negatywne; **positive reinforcement** wzmocnienie pozytywne; **vicarious reinforcement** wzmocnienie zastępcze

reinforcer czynnik wzmacniający

relapse nawrót choroby

release wyzwalać

relief ulga

relieve łagodzić, uśmierzać

remember (*syn.* **recall**, **recollect**) pamiętać, przypominać (sobie)

remind przypominać

remission remisja, nawrót

replay odtwarzać

repress tłumić

repression wyparcie, represja

reprieve ulga, wytchnienie

respiration oddychanie

response reakcja; **conditioned response** reakcja warunkowa; **unconditioned response** reakcja bezwarunkowa; **pupillary response** reakcja źrenic

restrictive eating restrykcyjne przestrzeganie diety

retain zatrzymywać, zachowywać (w pamięci)

retention zapamiętywanie, retencja

retina siatkówka

retinal degeneration zwyrodnienie siatkówki

retinoblastoma siatkówczak

retreat wycofywać się, uciekać

retrieval odzyskiwanie, wydobywanie

reverse odwracać, cofać

revise powtarzać; korygować

rhinorrhea nieżyt nosa

rod pręcik

rupture pęknięcie

S

salivate ślinić się

salivation ślinienie się

sanguine krew; sangwiniczny

saturation nasycenie, saturacja

schedule rozkład (wzmacniania); **fixed-interval schedule** rozkład wzmacniania o stałych odstępach czasowych; **fixed-ratio schedule** rozkład wzmacniania według stałych proporcji; **variable-interval schedule** rozkład wzmacniania o zmiennych odstępach czasowych; **variable-ratio schedule** rozkład wzmacniana według zmiennych proporcji

schema (*plur*. **schemata**) schemat

schizophrenia schizofrenia

sedative (*syn*. **tranquiliser**) środek uspokajający

seizure atak, napad (choroby); **epileptic seizure** napad padaczkowy

self jaźń

self-destructive autodestrukcyjny

self-efficacy poczucie własnej skuteczności

self-esteem poczucie własnej wartości

self-fulfilling prophecy samospełniająca się przepowiednia

sensation czucie; doznanie, wrażenie

sense zmysł; **chemical sense** zmysł chemiczny; **sense of hearing** (*or* **audition**) zmysł słuchu, słuch; **sense of sight** (*or* **vision**) zmysł wzroku, wzrok; **sense of smell** (*or* **olfaction**) zmysł węchu, węch; **sense of taste** (*or* **gustation**) zmysł smaku, smak; **sense of touch** (*or* **tactition**) zmysł dotyku, dotyk

sensory czuciowy, sensoryczny, zmysłowy

severe (*syn*. **acute**) ostry

sexism seksizm, dyskryminacja ze względu na płeć

sexual drive popęd seksualny, popęd płciowy

sighted widzący

sizeism dyskryminacja ze względu na tuszę

skill umiejętność; **motor skills** umiejętności motoryczne, umiejętności ruchowe

skin skóra

skull czaszka

sleep (*n*.) sen; **non-REM sleep** sen nie-REM; **REM sleep** sen REM; **slow-wave sleep** sen wolnofalowy

sleep (*v.*) spać

sleep cycle cykl snu

sleep paralysis porażenie przysenne (również paraliż senny, paraliż przysenny)

sleep terrors (*or* **night terrors**) lęki nocne

sleeping pills leki nasenne

sleep-wake cycle cykl snu i czuwania

sleepwalking (*or* **somnambulism**) lunatyzm, somnambulizm

slip of the tongue przejęzyczenie, lapsus językowy

snore chrapać

snorting (*syn.* **snuffing**) wciąganie do nosa

snuffing (*syn.* **snorting**) wciąganie do nosa

social norm norma społeczna

social withdrawal wycofanie społeczne

somatic somatyczny

somnambulism (*or* **sleepwalking**) lunatyzm, somnambulizm

somnolent (*syn.* **drowsy**) senny

spasm spazm, drgawka

speech mowa; **slurred speech** mowa zamazana; **telegraphic speech** mowa telegraficzna

spinal cord rdzeń kręgowy

spontaneous recovery samorzutne odnowienie

stage stadium, faza; **anal stage** faza analna; **concrete operational stage** stadium operacji konkretnych; **formal operational stage** stadium operacji formalnych; **genital stage** faza genitalna; **latency stage** faza latencji; **oral stage** faza oralna; **phallic stage** faza falliczna; **pre-operational stage** stadium przedoperacyjne; **sensorimotor stage** stadium sensomotoryczne

stapes (*or* **stirrup**) strzemiączko

stigma piętno

stimulant stymulant

stimulate stymulować, pobudzać

stimulus (*plur.* **stimuli**) bodziec; **conditioned stimulus** bodziec warunkowy; **external stimulus** bodziec zewnętrzny; **neutral stimulus** bodziec obojętny; **unconditioned stimulus** bodziec bezwarunkowy

stimulus generalisation generalizacja bodźca

stirrup (*or* **stapes**) strzemiączko

stool stolec

storage przechowywanie, magazynowanie

store wprowadzać do pamięci

strengthen wzmacniać

striatum prążkowie

stroke udar mózgu

subcortical podkorowy

subcutaneous tissue (*or* **hypodermis**) tkanka podskórna

sublimation sublimacja

substance substancja psychoaktywna

substitute (*n.*) zamiennik, substytut

substitute (*v.*) zastępować

suffer (from) cierpieć (na)

sufferer cierpiący

superego (*cf.* **id**, **ego**) superego, w psychoanalizie jeden z trzech komponentów osobowości

susceptibility (to) podatność (na)

sweat (*n.*) pot

sweat (*v.*) pocić się

sweat gland gruczoł potowy

synapse synapsa

syndrome syndrom, zespół; **Kleine-Levin syndrome/'sleeping beauty' syndrome** zespół Kleine'a-Levina/syndrom śpiącej królewny; **Korsakoff's syndrome** zespół Korsakowa; **restless legs syndrome (RLS)** zespół niespokojnych nóg; **savant syndrome** zespół sawanta

T

tactile (*syn.* **haptic**) dotykowy

tactition (*or* **sense of touch)** zmysł dotyku, dotyk

taste bud kubek smakowy

terminate przerywać, kończyć

termination przerwanie

thalamus wzgórze

the unconscious podświadomość

theory teoria; **multiple intelligences theory** teoria inteligencji wielorakiej; **psychoanalytic theory** teoria psychoanalityczna; **social cognitive theory** teoria społeczno-poznawcza; **threat simulation theory** teoria symulacji zagrożenia; **triarchic theory of intelligence** triarchiczna/triadowa teoria inteligencji

thought insertion nasyłanie myśli

thought myśl; **intrusive thoughts** natrętne myśli, natręctwa myślowe; **racing thoughts** natłok myśli, gonitwa myśli; **suicidal thoughts** myśli samobójcze

threshold próg; **absolute threshold** próg absolutny; **difference threshold** próg różnicy

timbre barwa dźwięku, tembr

toddler dziecko uczące się chodzić

tolerance tolerancja (farmakologiczna)

tongue język

trait cecha

tranquiliser (*syn.* **sedative)** środek uspokajający

transduce przetwarzać

transduction transdukcja

treatment leczenie

tremor drżenie, drganie

trigger wyzwalać, uruchamiać

twitch skurcz, drgawka

U

umbilical cord pępowina

umbilicus pępek

unconscious nieprzytomny

undiagnosed (*cf.* **misdiagnosed**) niezdiagnozowany

uninhibited niepohamowany, nieskrępowany, bez zahamowań

unstable niestabilny, zmienny, chwiejny

urge pragnienie

uterine maciczny

uterus (*or* **womb**) macica

utter wypowiadać, mówić

utterance wypowiedź, wyrażenie

V/W/Y/Z

vague (*syn.* **blurry**) mglisty, niewyraźny, niejasny

vanish zanikać

vent (sth on sb) wyładowywać (coś na kimś)

vertebrate kręgowce

vibrate drgać, wprawiać w drganie

vibration drganie

viral wirusowy

virus wirus

vision (*or* **sense of sight**) zmysł wzroku, wzrok; **colour vision** widzenie barwne; **distance vision** widzenie dali

visual wzrokowy, wizualny

visual acuity (VA) ostrość wzroku

vocabulary spurt eksplozja słownictwa

vowel samogłoska

vulnerable (to) podatny, narażony (na)

waking czuwający

wavelength długość fali

weaken osłabiać

wean odstawiać od piersi

webaholic osoba uzależniona od Internetu

white cane biała laska (niewidomego)

withdrawal zespół odstawienia

withhold wstrzymywać

womb (*or* **uterus**) łono, macica

word order szyk wyrazów

word salad sałata słowna, schizofazja

workaholic pracoholik

yield dawać (wynik)

zygote zygota

Nowoczesne podręczniki
do języka angielskiego
Marzena Beata Hoszowska
International Business English in Everyday Use
Wydanie z płytą
płyta mp3 w środku
wydawnictwo
poltext
wydawnictwo
poltext
www.poltext.pl